Produced specifically for companies involved
in the sport, this book is one of only
500 issued for retail sale.

This page has been specifically designed to accommodate your personal message on your A4 Headed Notepaper.

of horseracing

a photographic essay
of horseracing
in all its moods

MOODS OF HORSERACING is published by Moods of Mann Limited

Thie-ny-Chibbyr, Surby, Isle of Man, IM9 6TA. Tel: 01624 835656. Fax: 01624 836055

Copyright © Moods of Mann Limited 1997

ISBN 1 901709 00 0

British Library Cataloguing-in-Publication Data

A catalogue record for this book is available from the British Library

All rights are reserved. No part of this publication may be reproduced or used in any form or by means graphic, electronic or mechanical, including photocopying, recording, taping or information storage and retrieval systems without the written permission of the publisher.

Great care has been taken throughout this book to ensure that all details are accurate. However, the publishers cannot accept responsibility for errors that may occur.

Joint Editors	Michael Ingram, Rick Tomlinson, Robin Bigland and William Eve
Contributing writer	Lord Oaksey
Captions	Michael Ingram and William Eve
Design & Layout	C E Marketing
Photographic Consultant	Rick Tomlinson
Printed by	Fulmar Colour Printing Company Limited

ACKNOWLEDGEMENTS

The editors would like to thank all those who have assisted in this publication, in particular, the sponsors and the photographers (especially all those who entered the amateur photographic competition), and Helen Howlett for her help 'Behind the Scenes'.

Half Title Page: Woodbine racetrack. Toronto.
PHOTOGRAPH: ALLSPORT / TODD WARSHAW

Title Page: Morning Walkouts. Kentucky.
PHOTOGRAPH: ALLSPORT / SIMON BRUTY.

Copyright Page: Full gallop at Happy Valley.
PHOTOGRAPH: ALLSPORT / DAVE CANNON.

Contents Page: Newmarket dawn.
PHOTOGRAPH: TREVOR JONES.

Trust • Integrity • Service • Trust • Integrity • Service • Trust • Integrity • Service • Trust • Integrity • Service • Trust

Victor Chandler

CHANDLER HOUSE
17 LINHOPE STREET
LONDON NW1 6HT
TELEPHONE 0171 402 3500
FACSIMILE 0171 706 1238

Britain's No.1 Credit Bookmaker

Why not apply to be a part of our highly Confidential and Professional Service.

Our trained staff are always available for help and advice on opening a credit account.

Please call us on:
0171 402 3500
for more information

Represented at the rails at most major meetings

Vodafone.
The Premier Classic.

Right from the off Vodafone has headed the field in mobile communications here in the UK and around the world. With Vodafone everyone's on a winner.

VODAFONE·
YOU ARE NOT ALONE

Vodafone Limited, The Courtyard, 2-4 London Road, Newbury, Berkshire RG14 1JX.
Tel: +44 (0)1635 33251 Fax: +44 (0)1635 45713
http://www.vodafone.co.uk

contents

Introduction	11
Memories	12
The Dream	22
Behind the Scenes	32
Horses and Jockeys	60
The Spectators	84
The Betting	112
The Race	122
Victors and Vanquished	162
At the End of the Day	178
Sponsors of Moods of Horseracing	191

PHOTOGRAPH: ALLSPORT / DAN SMITH.

A WINNING TREBLE

United Racecourses run three of the most successful tracks in the country - Epsom, Kempton and Sandown. As a result, our racegoers are rewarded with a rich variety of racing throughout the year.

There are the two main classic races at Epsom in June - The Derby and The Oaks, Kempton's jumping epic - the King George VI Chase on Boxing Day, not to mention the unique, mixed Whitbread Gold Cup meeting at Sandown in April.

The quality of business entertaining opportunities on offer is without equal - as are the range of sponsorship opportunities at all three courses.

To find out more, or to arrange a visit to view the facilities, call

01372 470047

| EPSOM | KEMPTON | SANDOWN |

A Good Deal Racier

The Sporting Life

The triumph

The sadness

The fun

THE sport

Every day the great pictures of a great sport

The Sporting Life

INTRODUCTION

by Sir Thomas Pilkington Bt.,
Senior Steward of the Jockey Club

Nothing inspires the full gamut of emotions more than horseracing and the wonderful range of pictures in this book gives a real flavour of the mixture of drama, triumph, frustration, beauty, despair and intense excitement which go to make up that consuming passion generated by the thoroughbred racehorse.

The inherent love of animals, which is part of the British nature, finds expression in the hero worship bestowed on certain racehorses. It is a strength of feeling which, except in a very few cases, is not accorded to their owners, trainers or jockeys.

Horseracing is big business, giving employment to many thousands and generating significant income for the Government. It provides wonderful entertainment, from the glamour of the Royal Meeting at Ascot, to the courage and gritty determination of National Hunt racing on a small course in February.

However, at the heart of it all, and this is something we must never forget, is the horse. As the late John Hislop wrote, "On the Turf there is only one rightful king - the racehorse; and if he is not served in the manner due to him, neither he, nor his kingdom will prosper."

This excellent book serves him very well.

Sir Thomas Pilkington Bt.
The Senior Steward of the Jockey Club

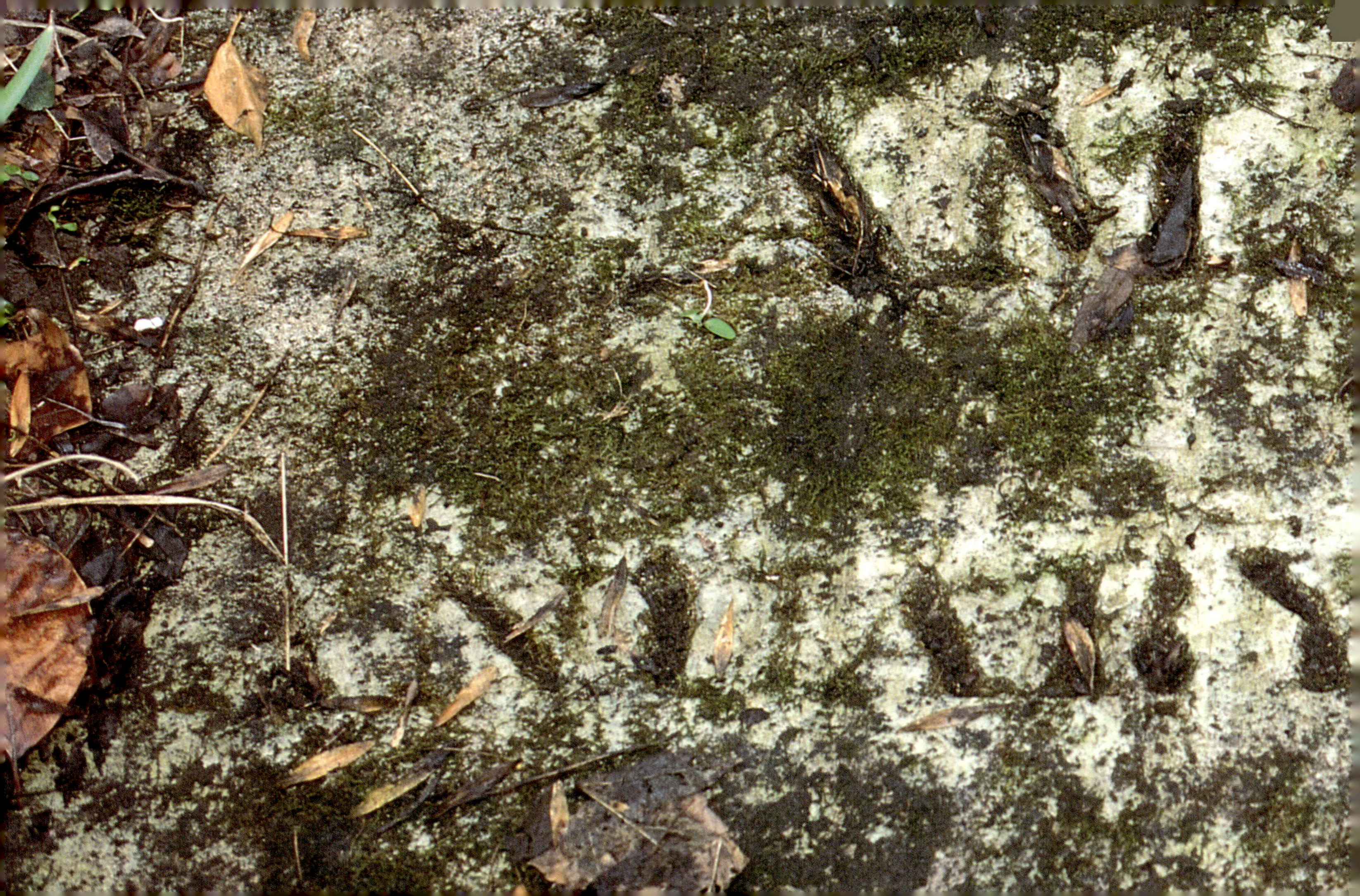

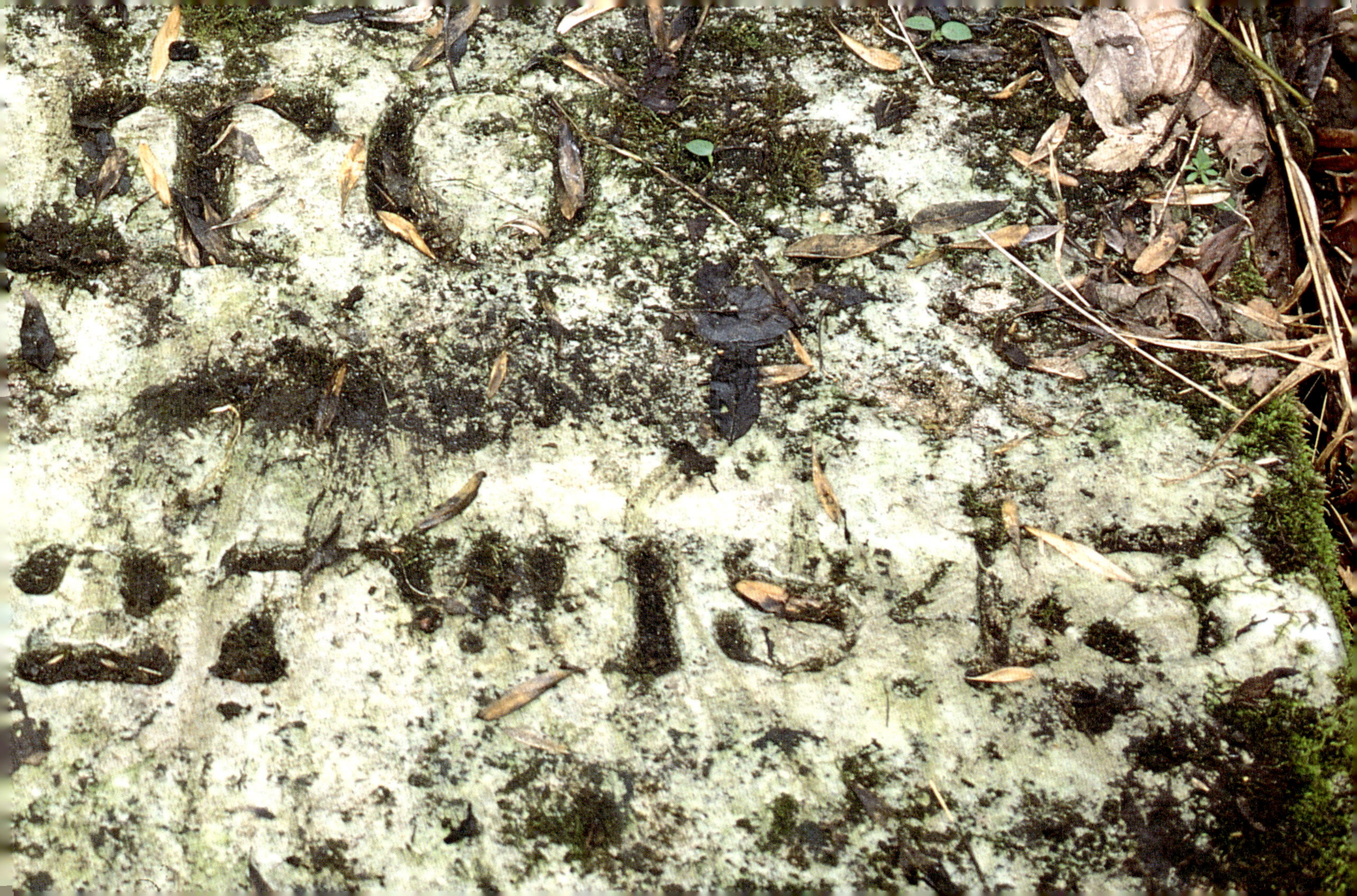

IN THE BUSINESS WORLD, AS IN THE WORLD OF RACING, COMPETITION IS HIGH. THE FUNDAMENTAL OBJECTIVE IS TO STAY AHEAD OF THE FIELD.

As a **PUBLICITY VEHICLE** and **MARKETING MEDIUM** horserace sponsorship has the ability to **KEEP YOU AHEAD OF THE FIELD**

NUMEROUS on-course branding and promotional opportunities

EXCLUSIVE right to the race name

EXTENSIVE press and media coverage

A CAPTIVE audience of almost **5 MILLION RACEGOERS** and **100 MILLION T.V. VIEWERS** annually…

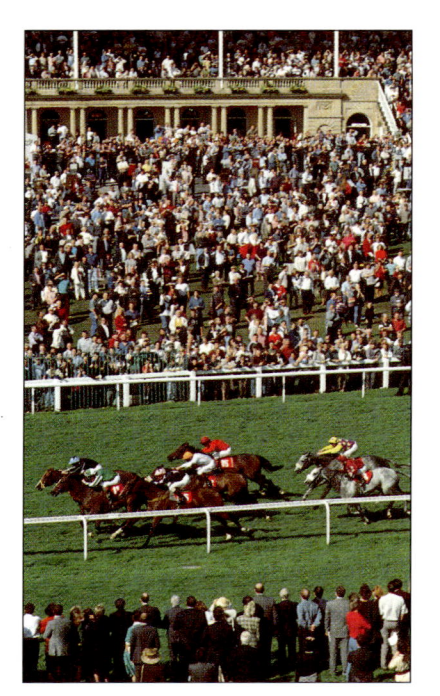

…producing **MAXIMUM EXPOSURE AT COMPARATIVELY LITTLE COST.**

Few other sporting events can match the excitement, anticipation, expectancy and sheer involvement of a day at the races. In addition to sponsorship, horseracing offers the perfect venue for corporate hospitality on any scale.

Weatherbys has been an integral part of British racing since 1770. Our close association with all of Britain's 59 racecourses, coupled with our sponsorship experience and dedication to the sport, will ensure that you get a sponsorship and corporate hospitality package to suit your requirements and budget.

For further information on sponsorship or corporate hospitality at any of Britain's 59 racecourses, please contact Julie Dyckhoff or Justyn Christer at:
WEATHERBYS GROUP LIMITED, SANDERS ROAD, WELLINGBOROUGH, NORTHAMPTONSHIRE NN8 4BX
TELEPHONE: 01933 440077   FAX: 01933 270300

No-one knows exactly when men first used horses to get from A to B.

But the horse is such an efficient - and handsome- form of transport that, without much doubt, he soon became a status symbol just as the car is now. Thereafter you can bet that in less time than it takes to say six to four, one proud horse owner decided to prove that his could go faster than anyone else's.

We know the Romans raced in Britain, even if they preferred Ben Hur-style chariots. The garrisons at Chester and York certainly amused themselves at the races and, by the 16th century, a Silver Ball, value three shillings and sixpence was offered as "The reward of speedy runnings" each year on Chester's Roodeye.

Between 1680 and 1730 the British 'invented' the thoroughbred - by buying (some say stealing) the three Arab stallions from whom the world's thoroughbreds are now descended. By that time the Royal Family, notably James 1 and Charles 11, had 'adopted' Newmarket and the sport was indelibly printed on the soul of our national life.

Previous pages: The grave of Amato. Derby winner in 1843.
PHOTOGRAPH: MICHAEL INGRAM.

Right: Golden Miller.
PHOTOGRAPH: TREVOR JONES.

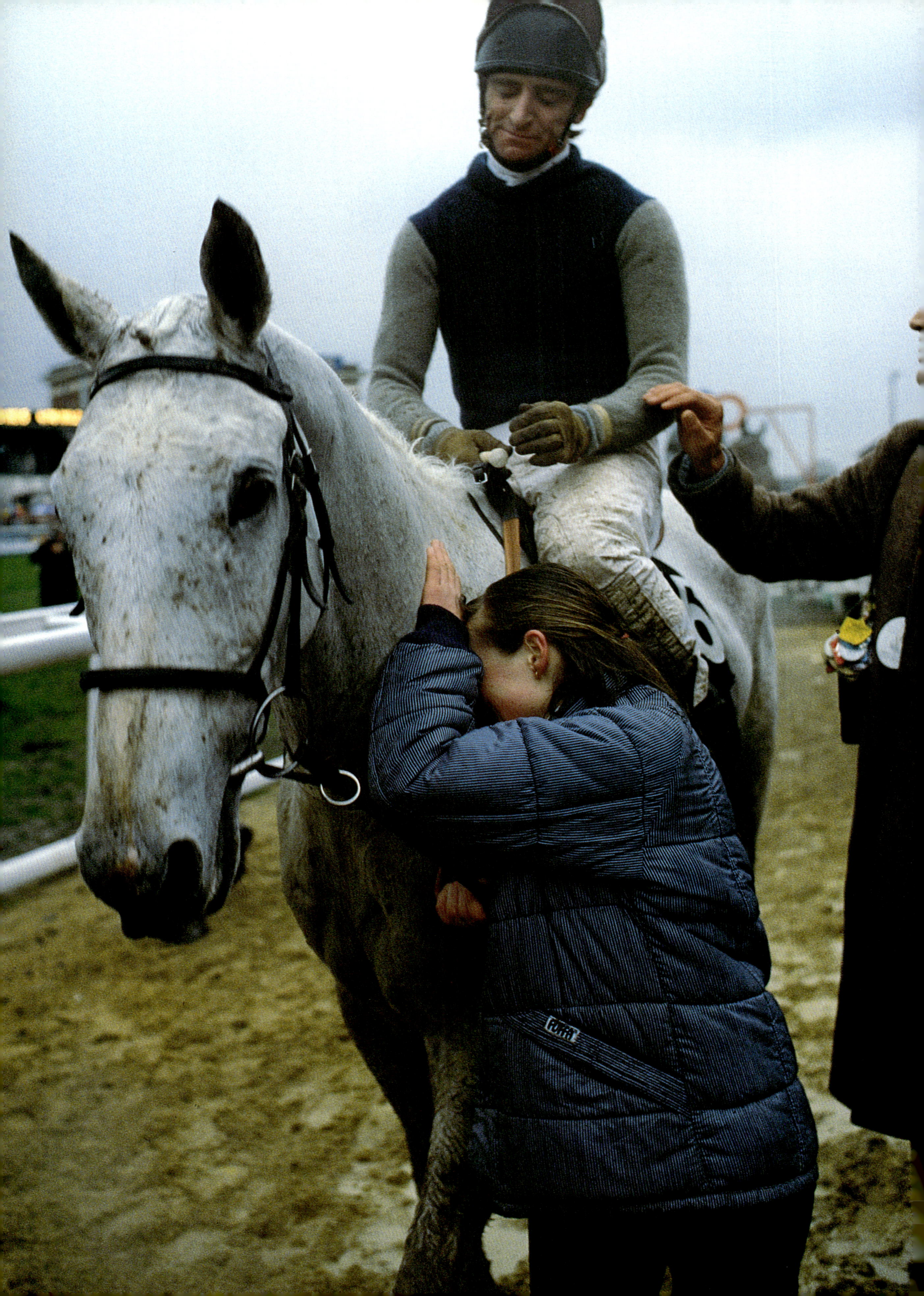

Above: Red Rum

Far Left: Desert Orchid.

Left: Mill Reef.
ALL PHOTOGRAPHED BY: TREVOR JONES

Below: A hero rests.
PHOTOGRAPH: STEPHEN GILMORE..

Above: Piggott and Eddery join the CID!
PHOTOGRAPH: AIDAN DULLAGHEN.
(WINNER OF THE CHAPTER CATEGORY).

Top Right: 'Derby Day, 1892, The Preliminary Canter'.
PHOTOGRAPH COURTESY OF THE ILLUSTRATED LONDON NEWS.

Middle Right: The 1967 Stable-lads Boxing finals.
PHOTOGRAPH COURTESY OF: BILLY HOWLETT.

Right: Lethal-looking spurs of the past. (Courtesy South Hatch Racing Museum).
PHOTOGRAPH: MICHAEL INGRAM.

Far Right Main Photo: The Race Board at The Curragh.
PHOTOGRAPH: AIDAN DULLAGHEN.

Far Right Inset: Great odds in 1949!
PHOTOGRAPH: BRENDA BROWN.

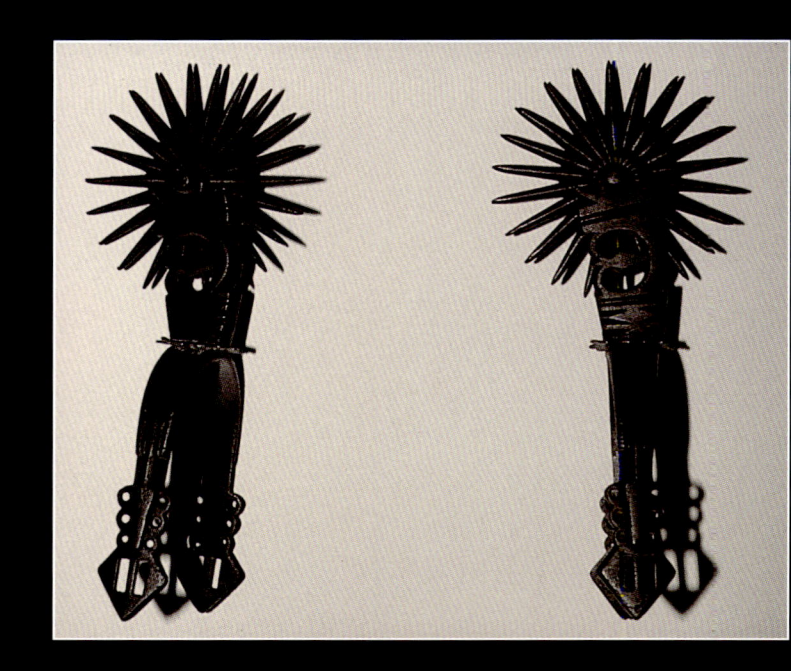

RACE 6
1 G.CURRAN 18
2 M.J.KINANE 17
3 C.ROCHE 1
4 L.PIGGOTT 10
5 D.GILLESPIE 14
6 P.EDDERY 16
7 S.MARTINEZ 4
8 J.DEEGAN 3
9 R.CARROLL 5
10 K.J.MANNING 9
12 G.McGRATH 8
13 J.T.HYDE 6
14 D.MANNING 11
15 N.CONNOLLY 12
16 P.BRAIDEN 15
17 P.LOWRY 2
18 J.MORGAN 7
GOING SOFT
DICK BROWN
VICTORIA CLUB
LIVERPOOL
Chester Cup
DICK BROWN

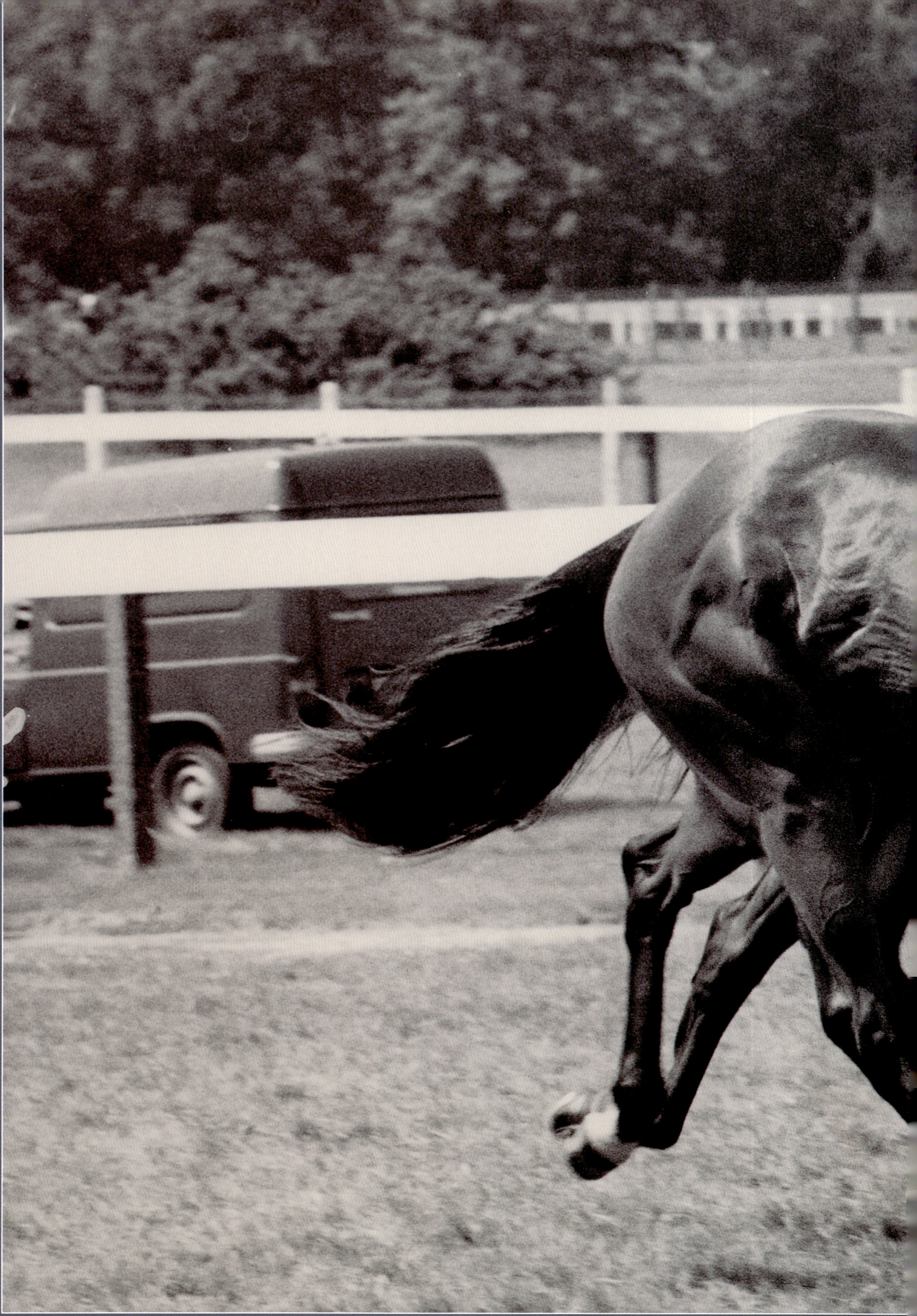

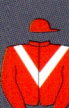

Did they really have six legs in those days?
PHOTOGRAPH: W EVERITT.

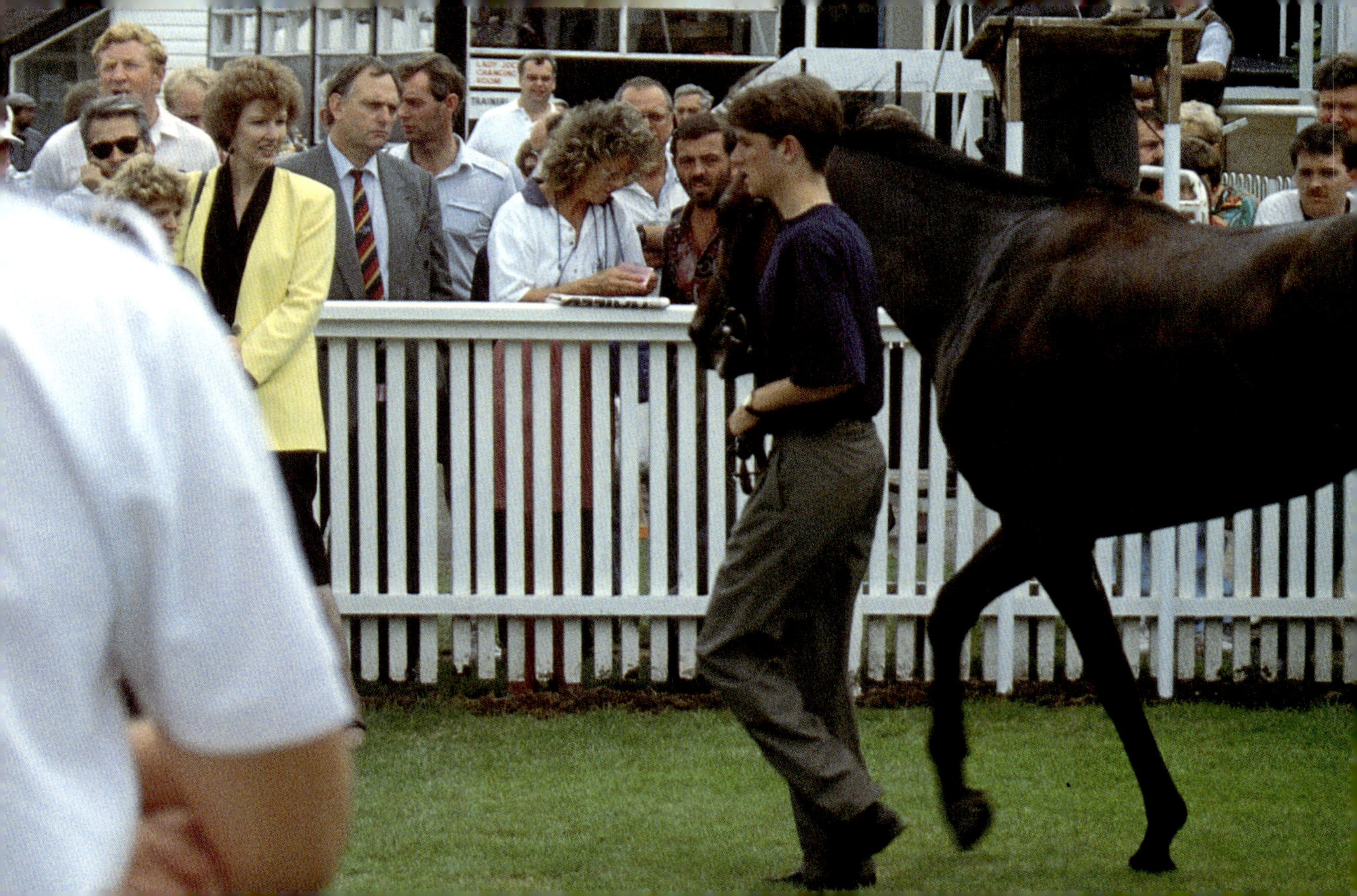

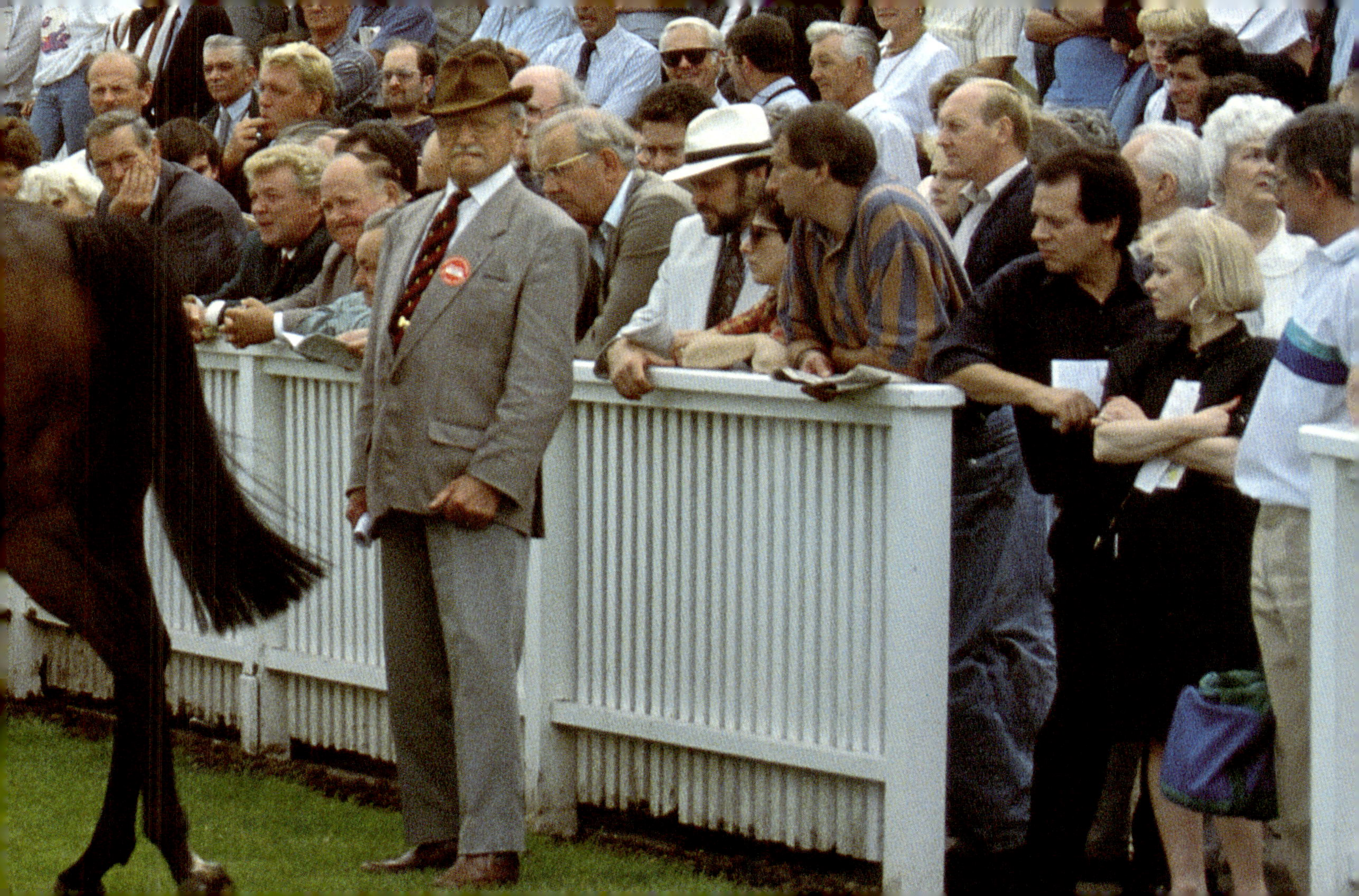

MAKING HEADLINES

AS OWNERS
Leading English-based owners with earnings of over **£3,000,000**

AS BREEDERS
Breeders of **8** individual Group race winners in 1996,
including Royal Ascot winners **PIVOTAL** and **DAZZLE**

AS VENDORS
Vendors of a Group **1** winner in each of the last 6 seasons *(1991/6)*
Leading vendors at the 1995 Houghton Sales

AS ONE OF EUROPE'S MAJOR STALLION STUDS
Currently home of leading European sires **POLAR FALCON**,
PRIMO DOMINIE, **PRINCE SABO**, **RUDIMENTARY** and **SADDLERS' HALL**,
and exciting prospects **BISHOP OF CASHEL** and **PIVOTAL**

Cheveley Park Stud
Duchess Drive, Newmarket, Suffolk CB8 9DD.
Telephone: 00 44 1638 730316. Fax: 00 44 1638 730868.

Glory means much less to a horse than food and a warm bed.

So you cannot train thoroughbreds like humans - using the dream of gold medals, fame and fortune to make the pain of hard work bearable. But strenuous exercise is still needed to get horses fit. So, since rolling hills build muscles and develop lungs, the downland training grounds of Britain are a landscape artist's dream.

Race meetings, often on far-off courses, happen in the afternoon. So, for the horses and their human handlers, a working day starts early.

First feed before dawn and on to the gallops before the mist has cleared. Nothing removes a hangover faster than having your arms pulled out - and although "Morning glories" don't always go quite so gloriously fast in the afternoon, the gallops are where most racing dreams are born.

Jockeys have to wake up early too - often driving miles before breakfast (if any) to test a horse's fitness or improve his jumping. Then off again by car or plane - to glory or despair in the afternoon.

Previous pages: Bidding for a winner.
PHOTOGRAPH: IAN YATES.

Above: Searching for a winner.
PHOTOGRAPH: ALLSPORT.

Above: "I'm going to follow in the footsteps of my father and grandfather
and become a Champion Trainer" says Tom Thomson Jones.
PHOTOGRAPH: JENNIFER UNDERWOOD.

Right: 'Watch out Lester...!
PHOTOGRAPH: JENNIFER UNDERWOOD.
(WINNER OF CHAPTER CATEGORY).

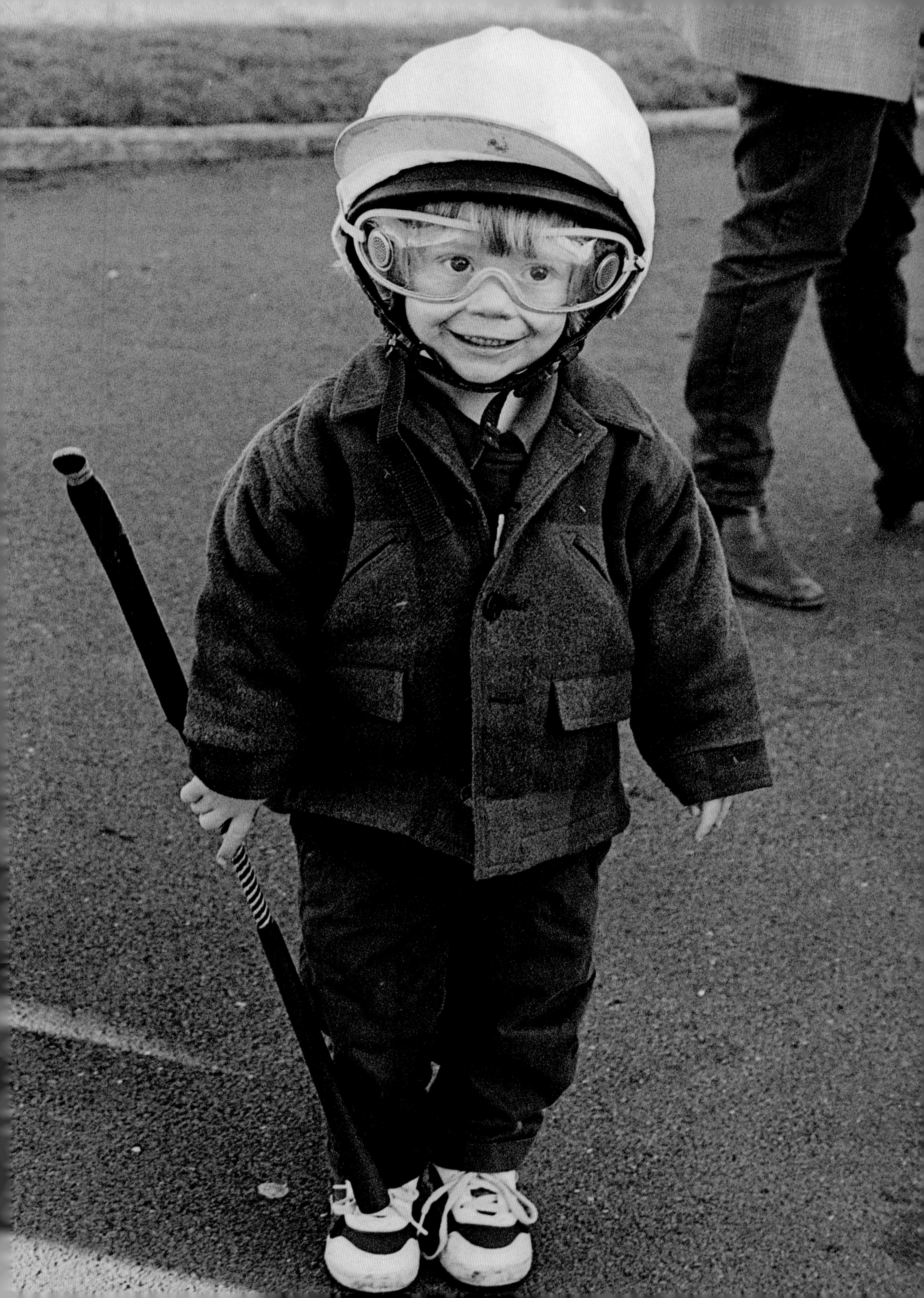

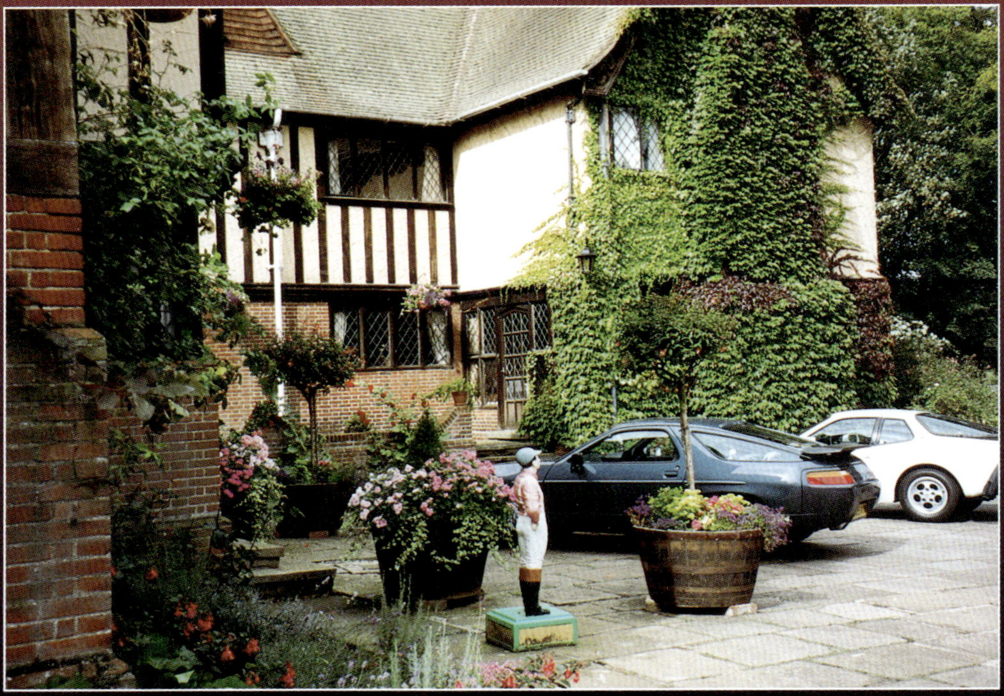

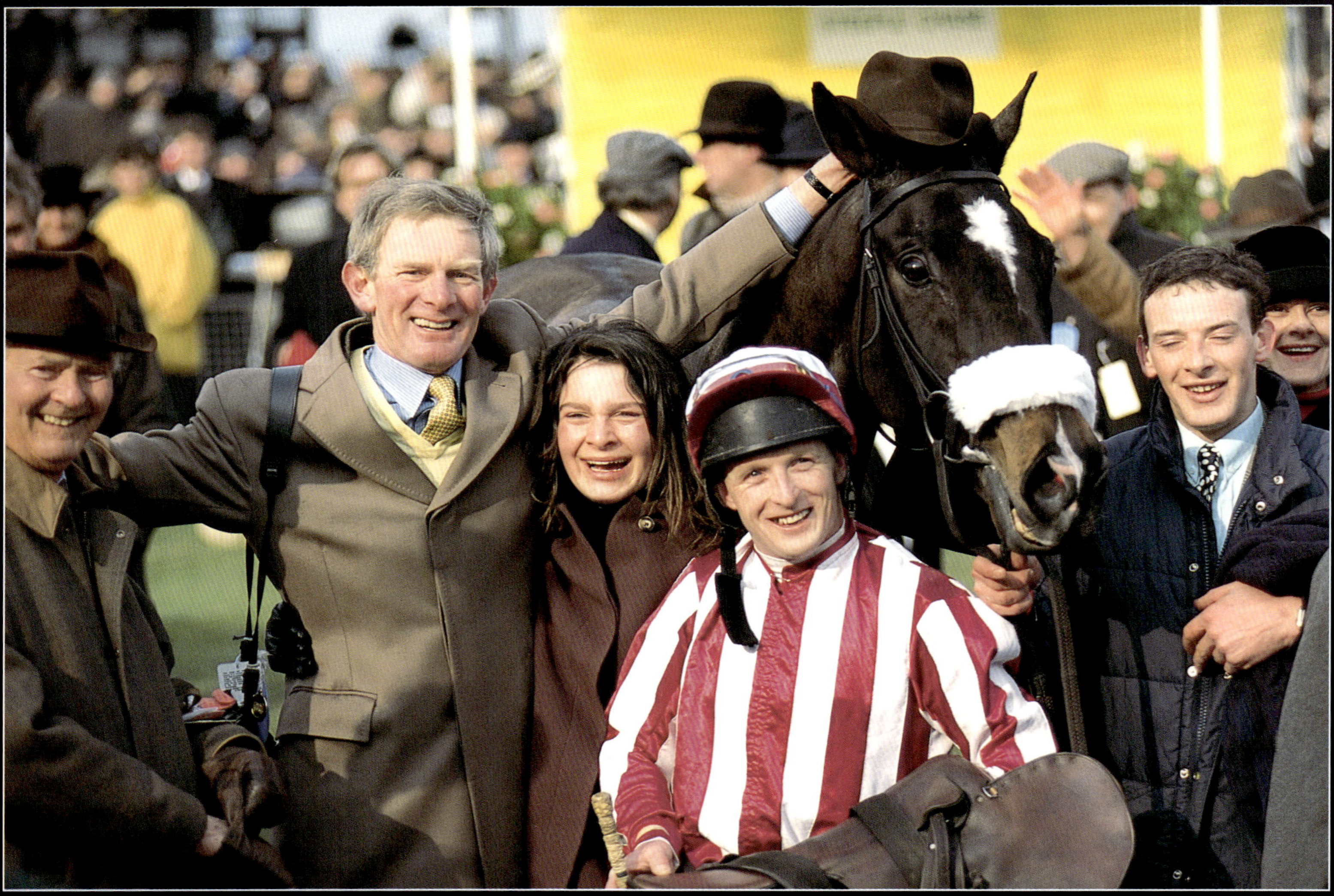

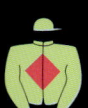

What dreams are made of...

Top Left: To the winner... the spoils.
PHOTOGRAPH: MRS P V PERKS.

Bottom Left: A winning team.
PHOTOGRAPH: TREVOR JONES.

Below: Joy.
PHOTOGRAPH: TREVOR JONES.

Right: One day I'm going to win the Derby!
PHOTOGRAPH: MISS L DAVIDGE.

Below: 'I'd rather be a horse…'
Remittance Man and stable companion.
PHOTOGRAPH: TREVOR JONES.

Thoroughbred Horseboxes

OLYMPIC
Coachbuilders Ltd

Milton Park • Abingdon • Oxon OX14 4SD • Telephone +44 (0)1235 861177 • Facsimile +44 (0)1235 862277

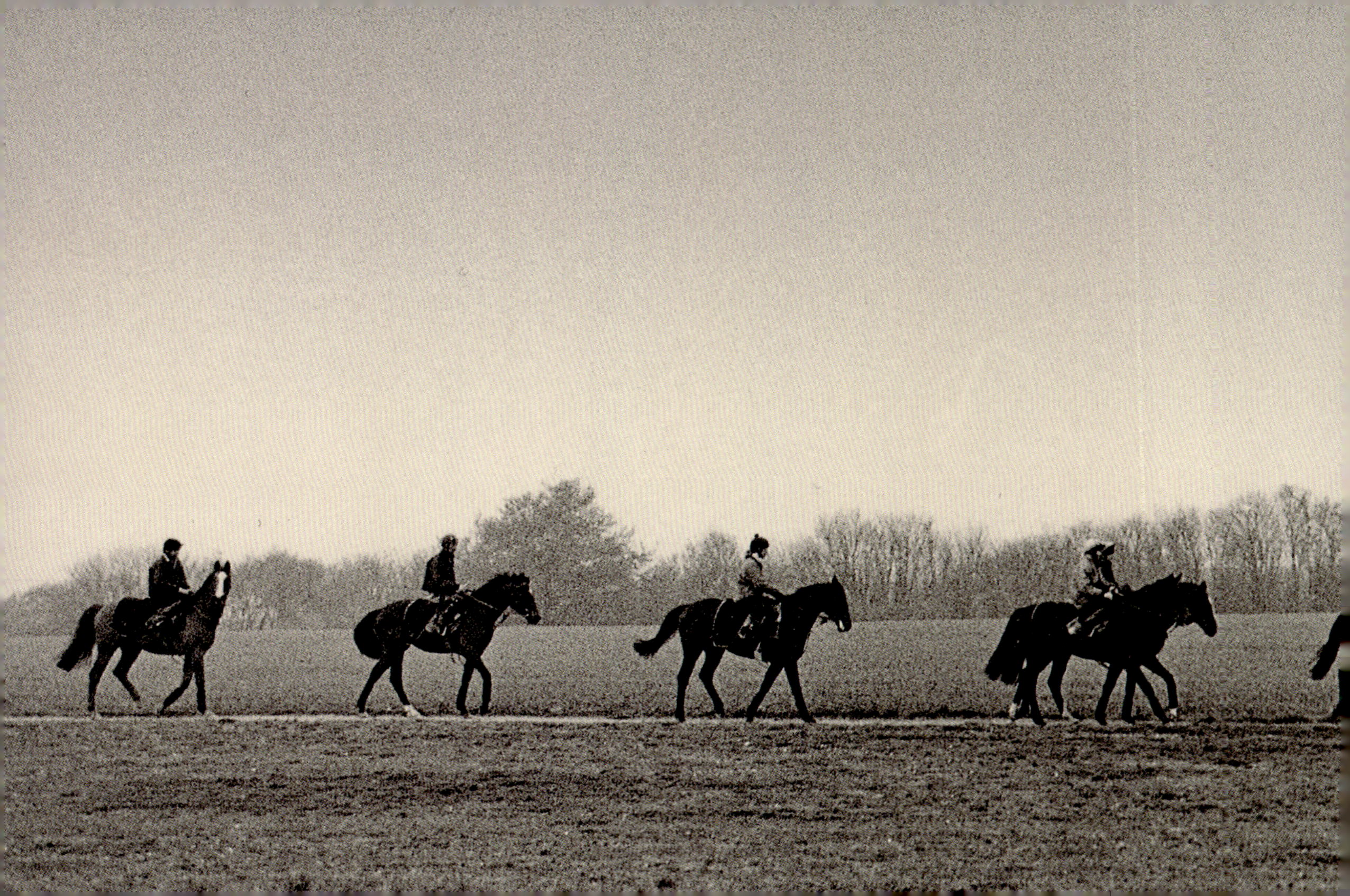

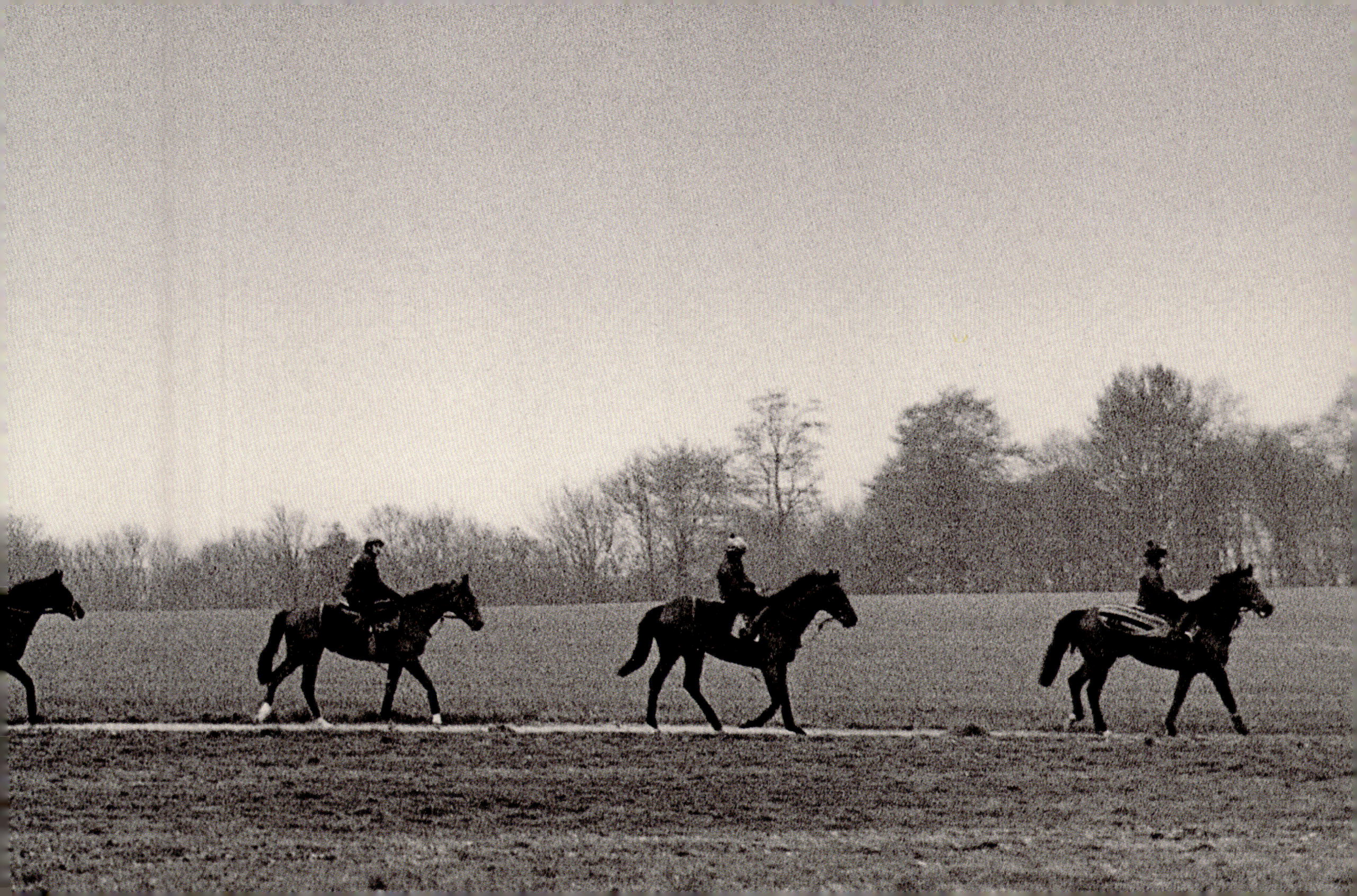

LETHEBY & CHRISTOPHER
AND
PAYNE & GUNTER

are proud to be Official Caterers to the country's premier racecourses:-

Aintree	Folkestone	Huntingdon
Ascot	Fontwell	Newmarket
Bath	Goodwood	Nottingham
Cheltenham	Hamilton Park	Plumpton
Chepstow	Haydock Park	Towcester
Chester		Windsor

For full details of corporate hospitality opportunities please call 0345 511 512 or fax 0345 298 299

There are still 50 racecourses in Britain

- far too many say those who claim the butter of Prize money is spread too thin. But variety is the spice of British racing. Courses vary from the splendour of Ascot, Cheltenham and York to Cartmel's tiny five-day roundabout or Fakenham's "Half way to Norway!"

Most stand empty, virtually unused for too much of the year. But each, great or small, becomes a stage - on which, for every actual raceday, the scene has to be laboriously set.

Not many courses nowadays could survive on gate money alone. Most depend heavily on the commercial sponsorship of races - and all are subsidised through the Levy Board, which gets its money from the punter. If betting stopped, let's face it, the whole expensive caravan would grind to an underfunded halt. So the Tote and bookies' stalls are even more vital than the sponsors' hoardings.

Previous pages: The string.
PHOTOGRAPH: JOHN CHASE.

Above: Silks.
PHOTOGRAPH: MICHAEL INGRAM.

Left: The Tack room.
PHOTOGRAPH: TREVOR JONES.

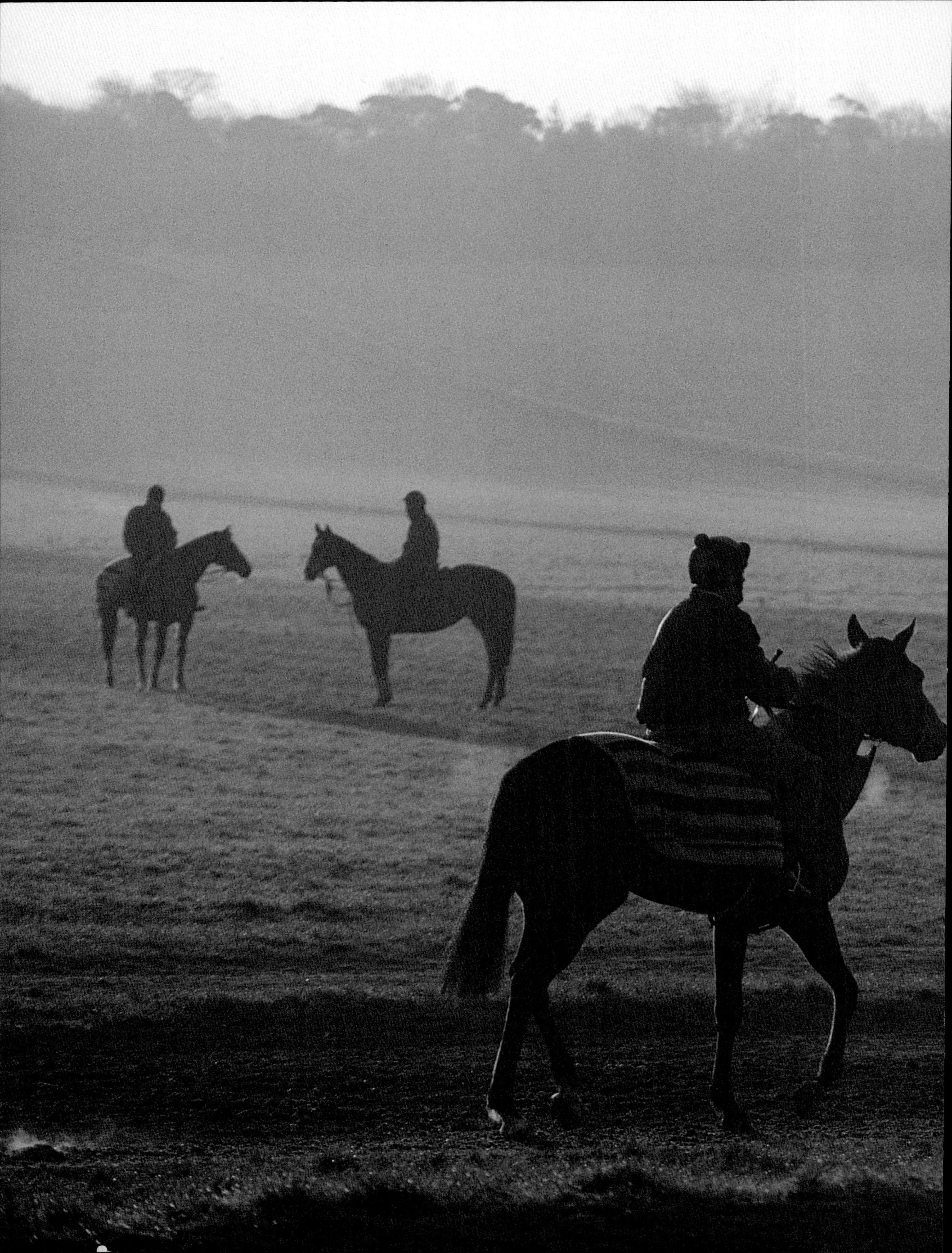

A Newmarket dawn.
PHOTOGRAPH: TREVOR JONES.

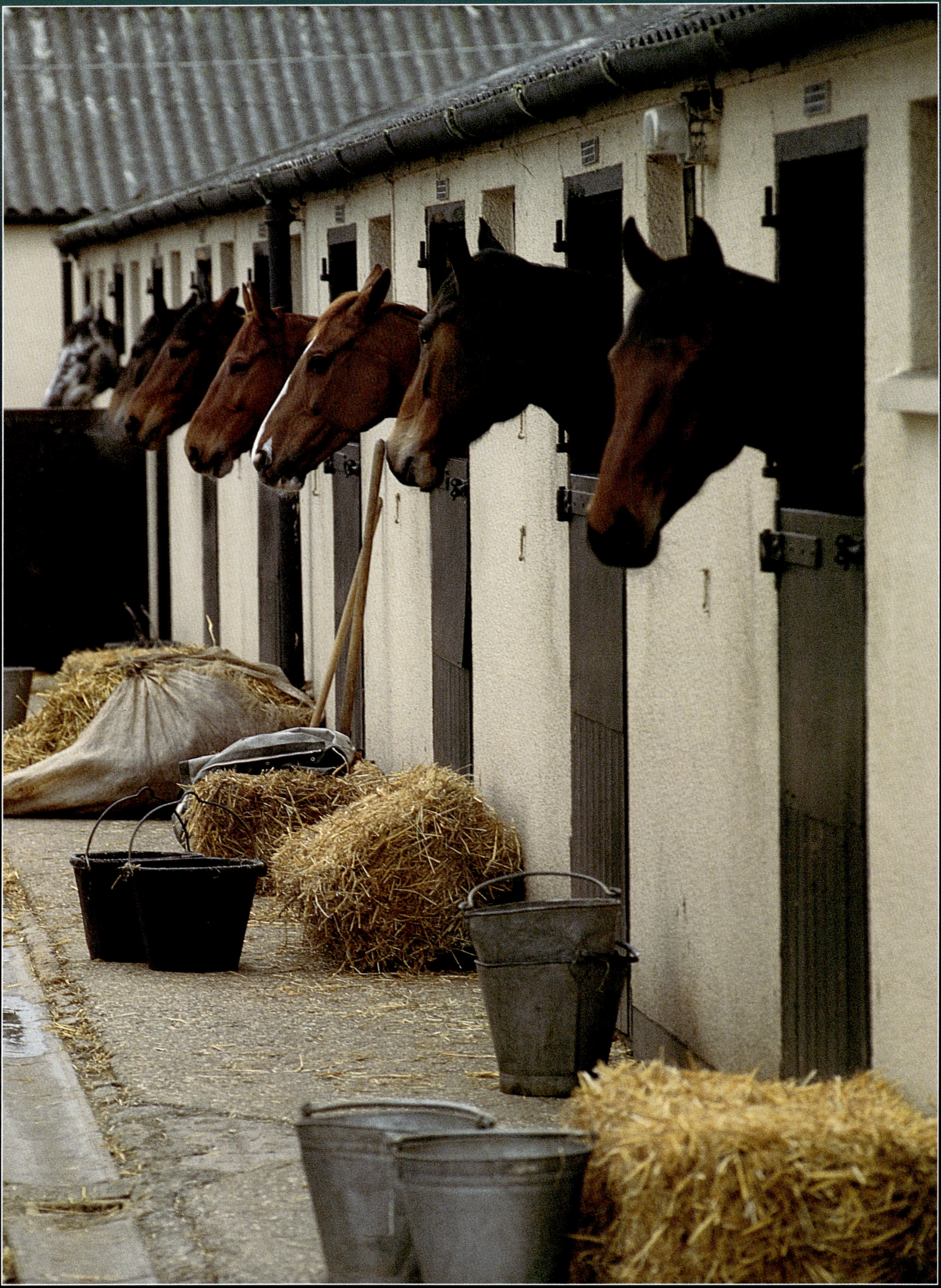

Left: Feed time approaches.
PHOTOGRAPH: TREVOR JONES.

Below: Returning from the gallops.
PHOTOGRAPH: TREVOR JONES.

Peter Chapple-Hyam's string at Manton.
PHOTOGRAPH: TREVOR JONES.

41

Top Left: A smithy at work.
PHOTOGRAPH: MRS P V PERKS.

Left: Preparing a mix of horse feed.
PHOTOGRAPH: MICHAEL INGRAM.

Above: Hosing down.
PHOTOGRAPH: KENNETH HARGREAVES.

Right: A horse-walker in use at Geoff Lewis' stables.
PHOTOGRAPH: WILLIAM EVE.

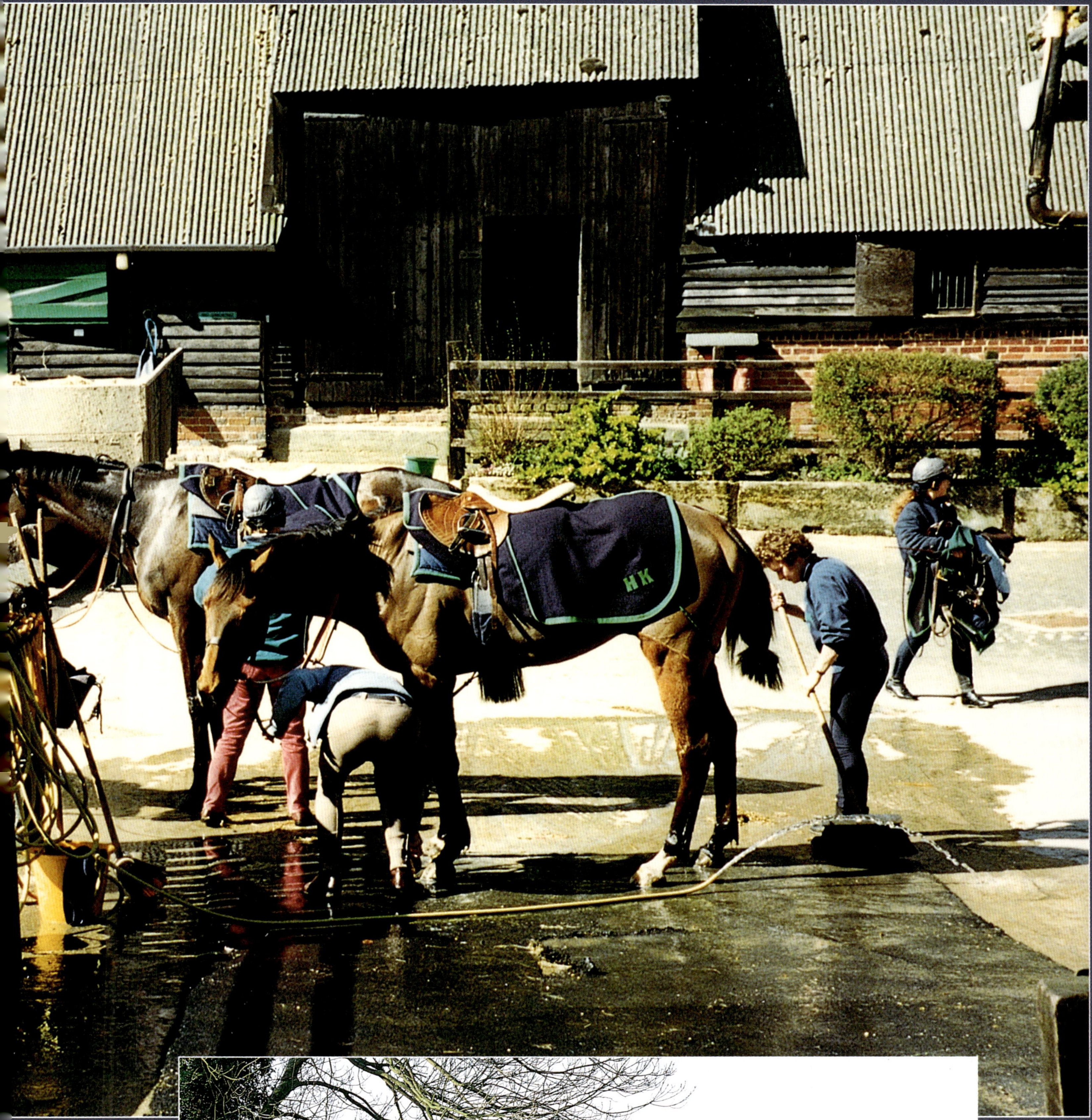
HK

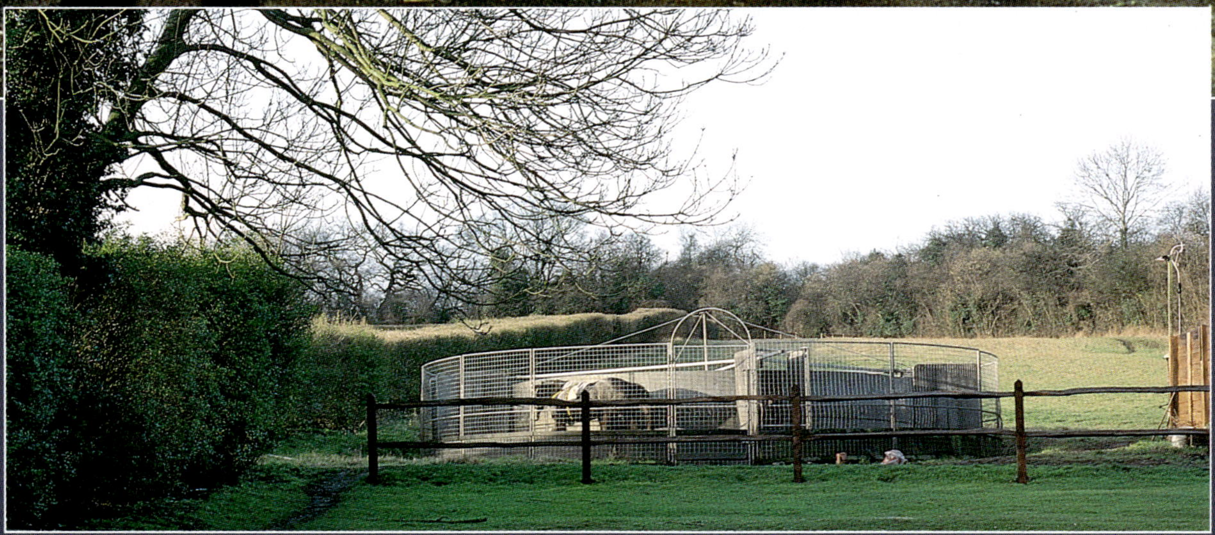

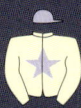

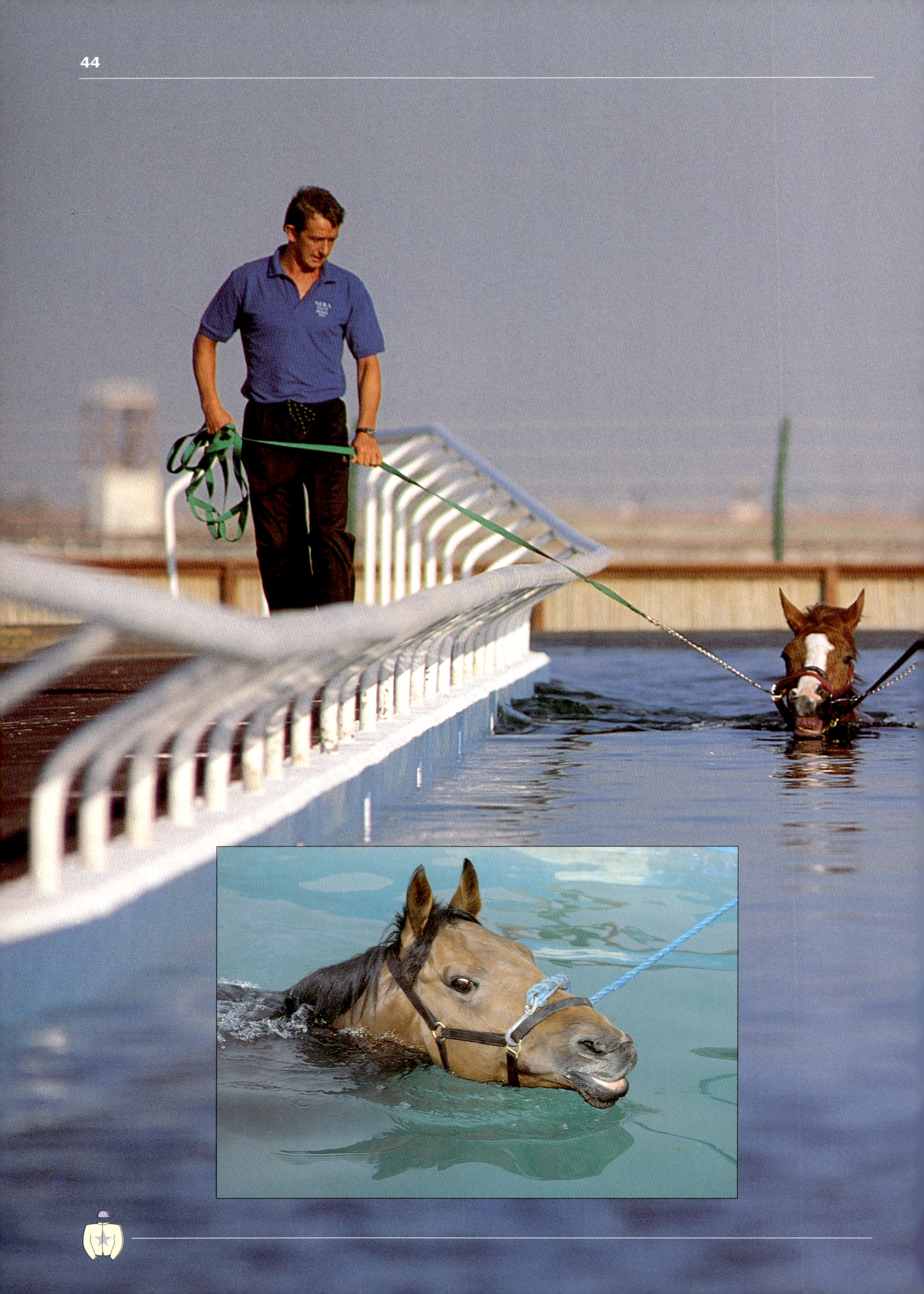

Equine pools are used to exercise horses and to help them back to full strength after injury.
PHOTOGRAPHS: TREVOR JONES.

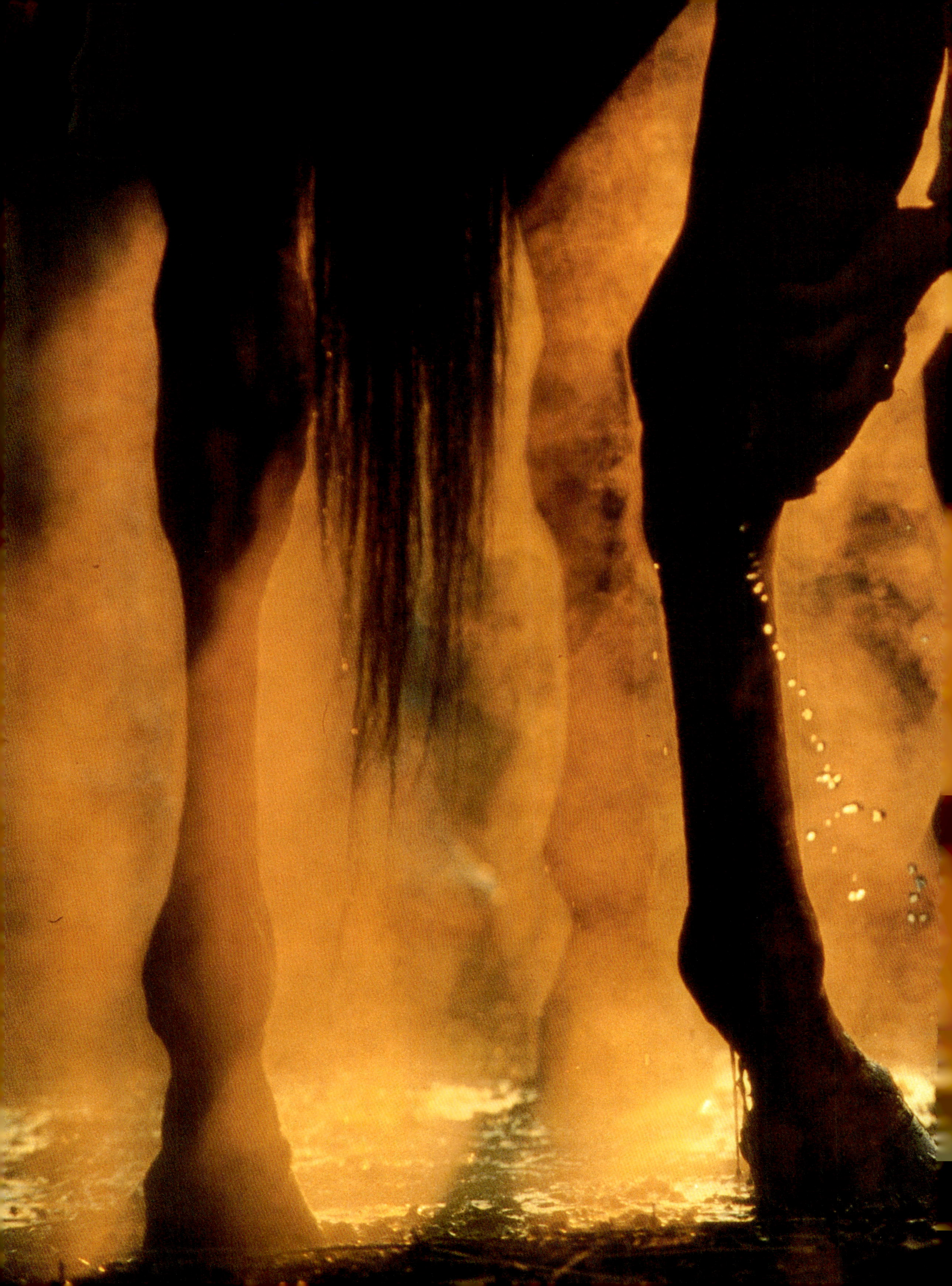

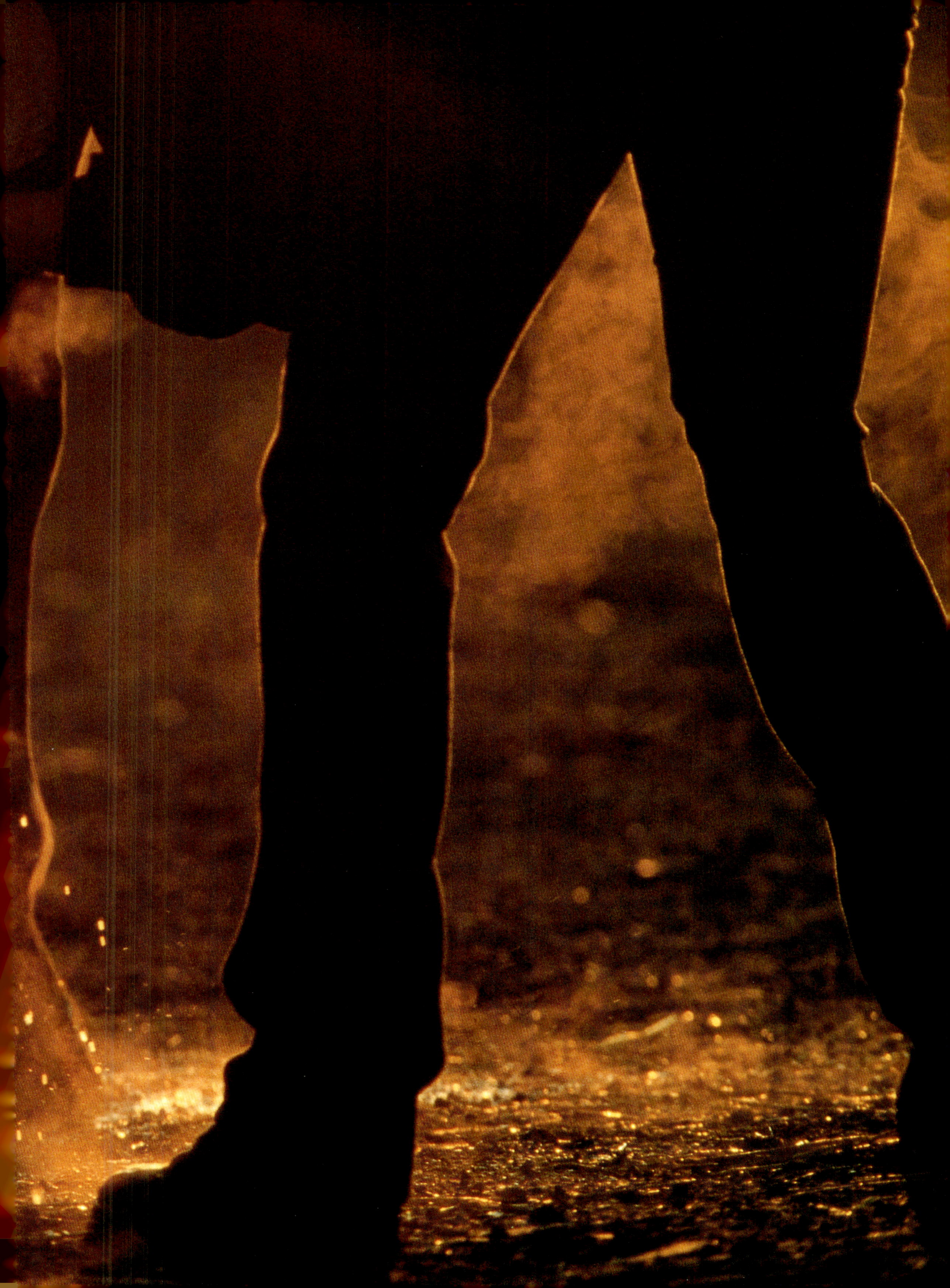

Previous pages: Hosing down after the Kentucky Derby.
PHOTOGRAPH: ALLSPORT / SIMON BRUTY.

Above: A stallion enjoys the freedom of the indoor training school at The Durdans, Epsom.
PHOTOGRAPH: MICHAEL INGRAM.

Right: A Japanese stud farm.
PHOTOGRAPH: ALLSPORT / ANTON WANT.

Next pages: Warren Hill. Newmarket.
PHOTOGRAPH: TREVOR JONES.

49

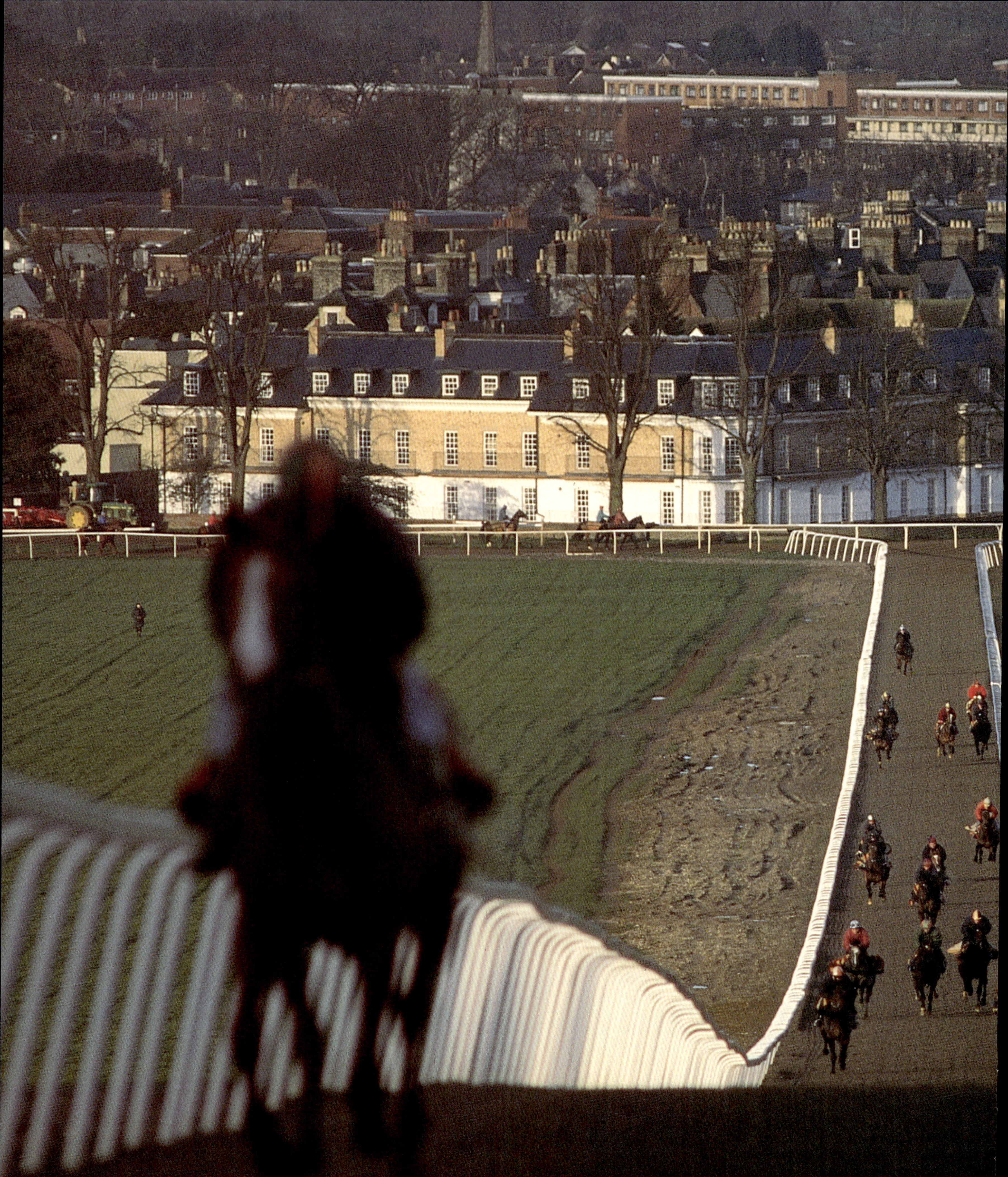

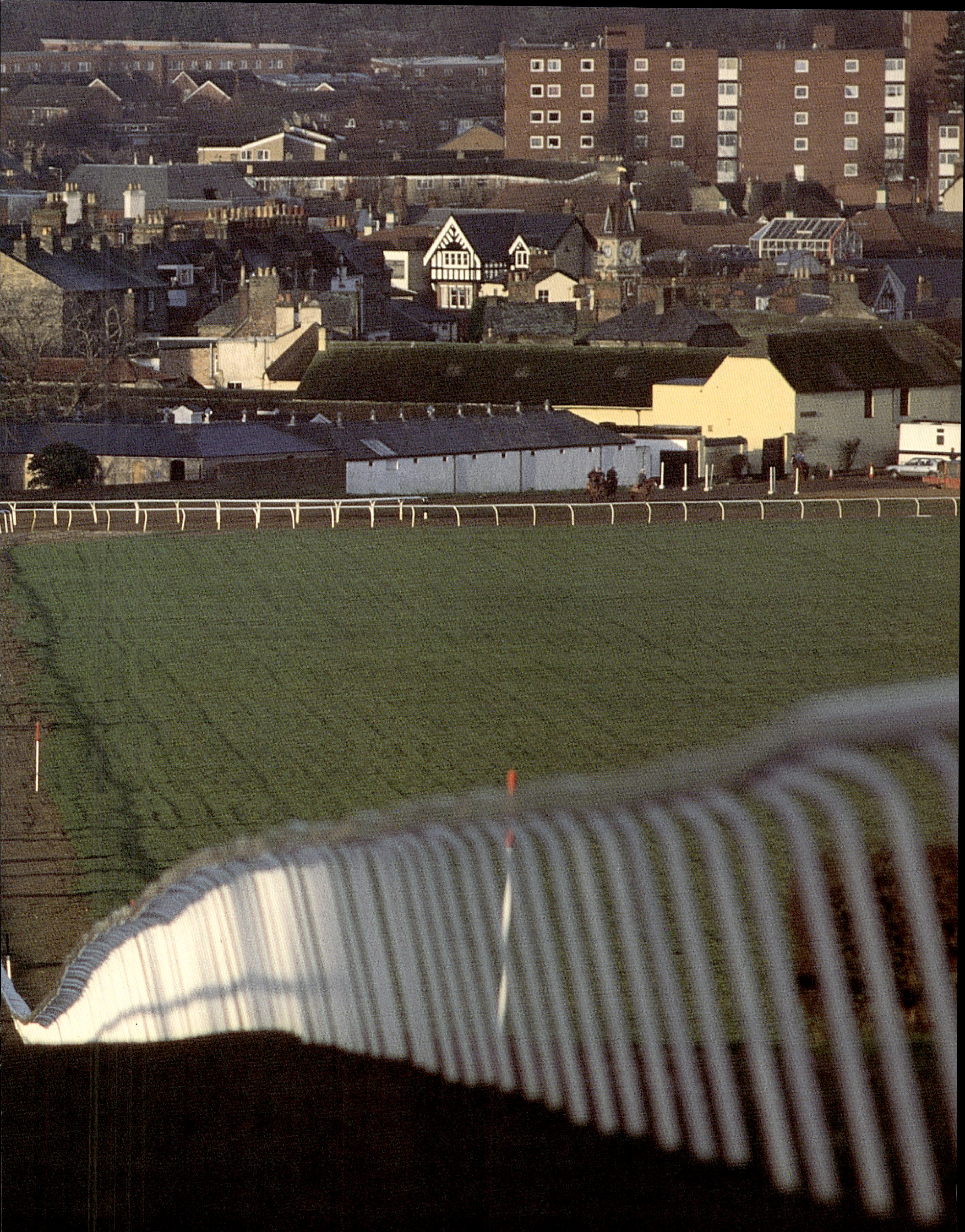

Top Left: Course distance markers.
PHOTOGRAPH: TREVOR JONES.

Left: "With grateful thanks…" Inspired by the injuries to Paddy Farrell and Tim Brook-Shaw, the Injured Jockeys' Fund's chief objective has always been to help jockeys whose lives are altered for the worst by the hazards of raceriding – especially those who are forced by injury to give up riding altogether.
PHOTOGRAPH: ROGER GOUGH.

Bottom left: Lady jockeys riding each other.
PHOTOGRAPH: TREVOR JONES.

Top Right: Many horses are transported by air to the various international meetings
PHOTOGRAPH: COURTESY LUFTHANSA.

Top Far Right: Fatherland arrives from Ireland.
PHOTOGRAPH: TREVOR JONES.

Bottom Right: A TV camera at Sandown Park.
PHOTOGRAPH: TREVOR JONES.

53

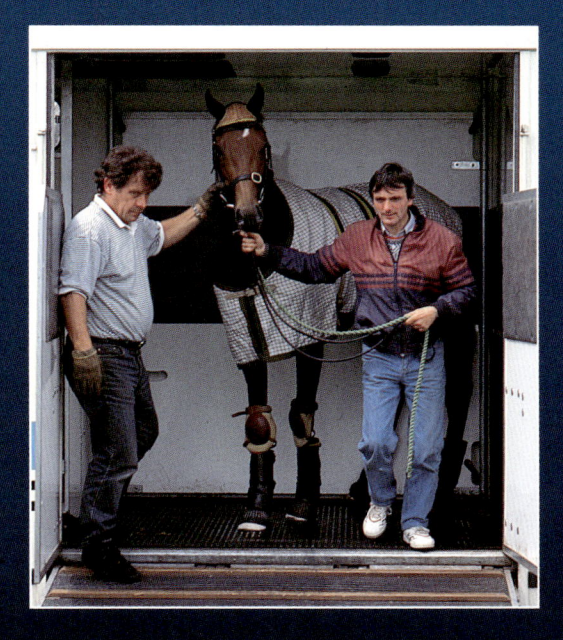

Above: George Moore's string.
PHOTOGRAPH: SUE ORPWOOD.
(WINNER OF THE CHAPTER CATEGORY).

Top Right: Winter scene.
PHOTOGRAPH: TREVOR JONES.

Right: Newmarket in January.
PHOTOGRAPH: TREVOR JONES.

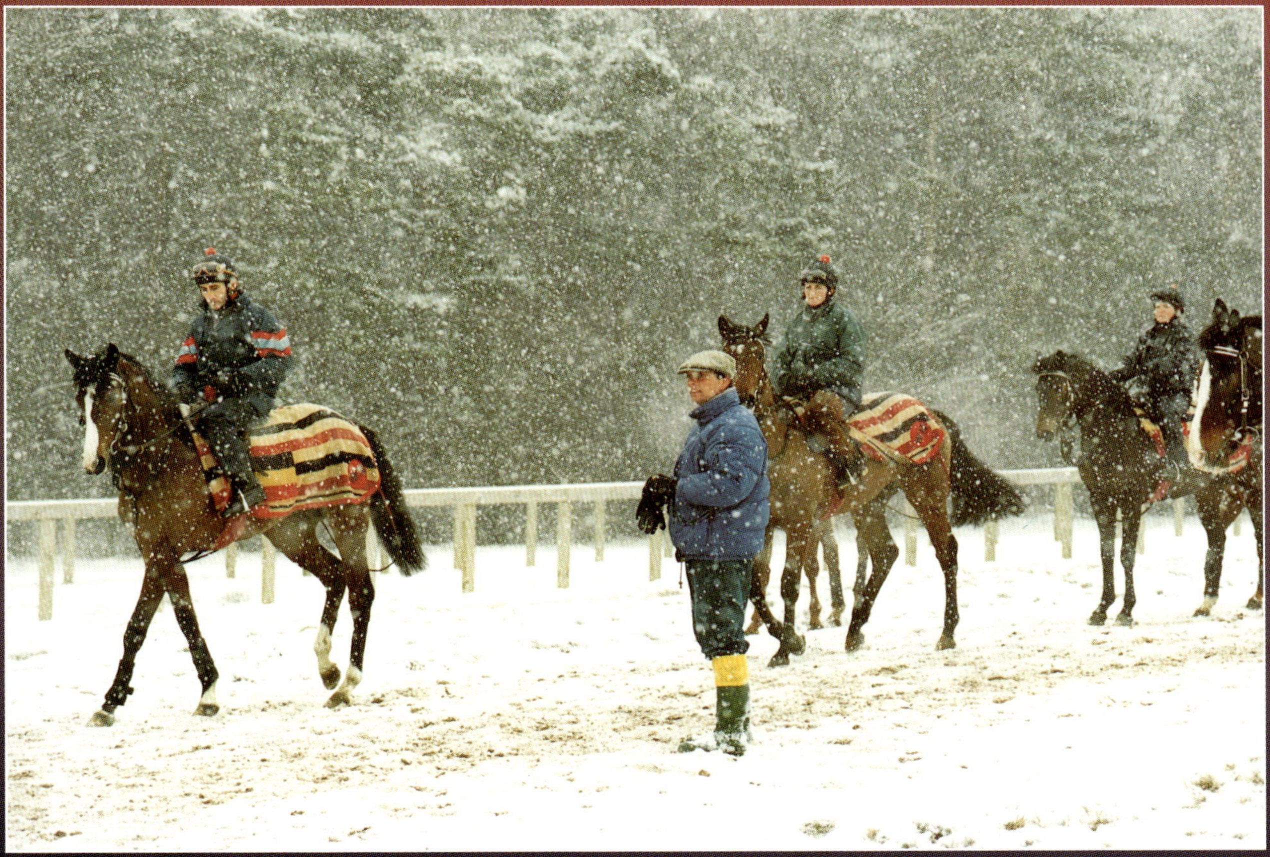

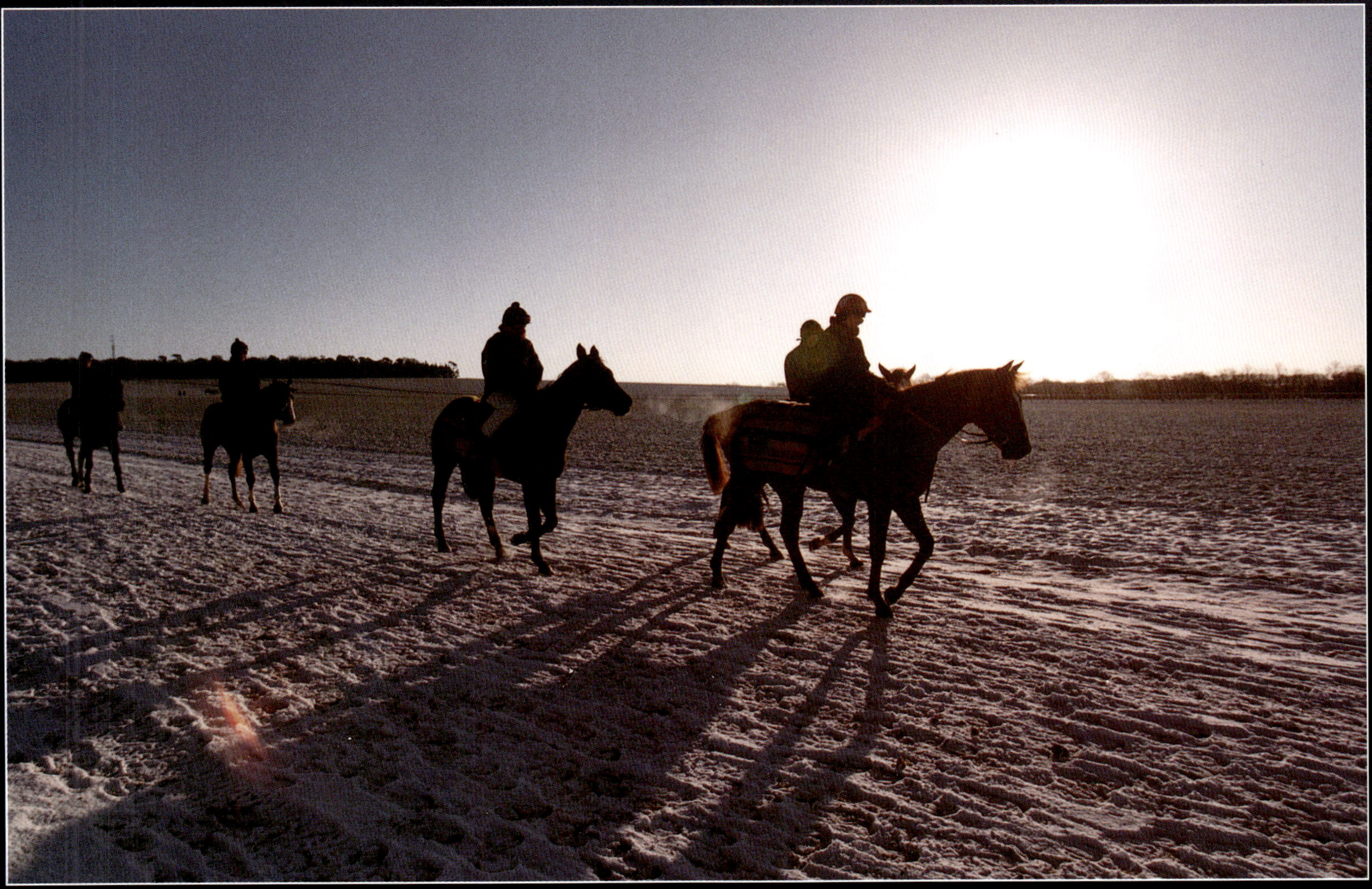

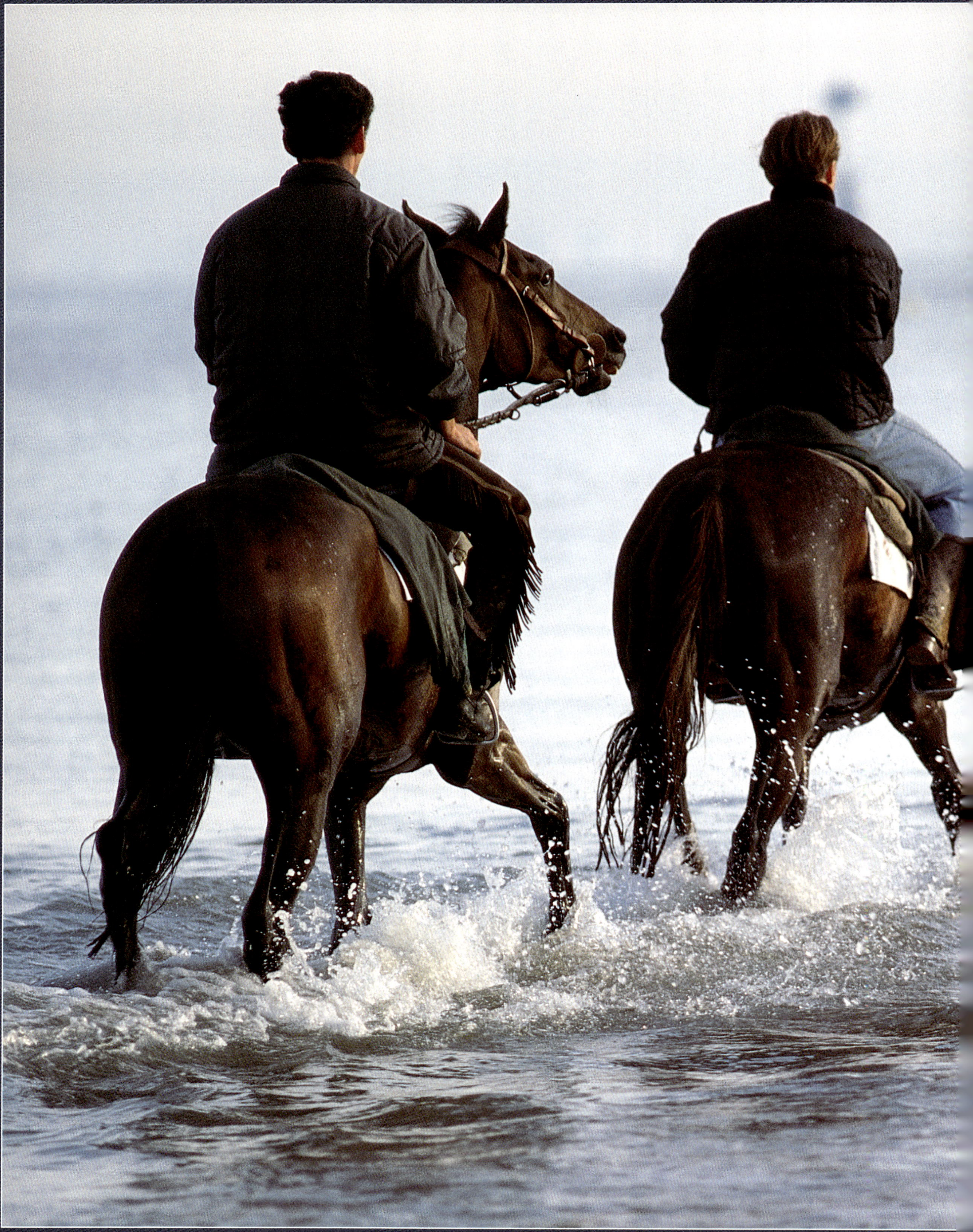

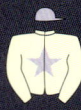

Exercising on Deauville beach.
PHOTOGRAPH: TREVOR JONES.

Left: Young horses get used to the starting stalls.
PHOTOGRAPH: TREVOR JONES.

Below: Warren Hill Gallop. Newmarket.
PHOTOGRAPH. POLYTRACK.

MARTIN COLLINS ENTERPRISES

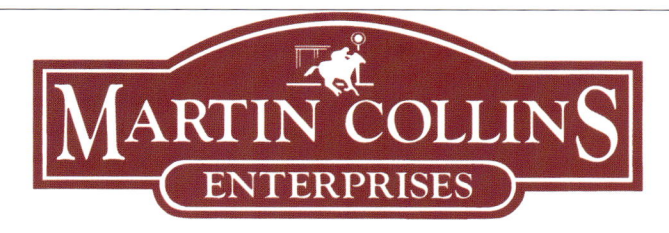

MANUFACTURERS AND INSTALLERS OF SYNTHETIC RIDING SURFACES FOR ARENAS AND GALLOPS

POLYTRACK   GELTRACK   PROTRACK
Britain's No.1 Synthetic Wax Coated Surfaces

EQUISAND   EQUICOURT   EQUIMIX
Tried and Tested - Still Going Strong

NEW WAXED EQUICOURT PVC GRANULES

NEW WAXED EQUISAND

RUBBER MATTING for stables, horseboxes & walk areas

Cuckoo Copse, Lambourn Woodlands, Hungerford, Berkshire RG17 7TJ
Telephone: 01488 71100   Fax: 01488 73177

Martin Collins with Peter Amos, General Manager, Jockey Club Estates at the Polytrack Al-Bahathri Gallop, Newmarket

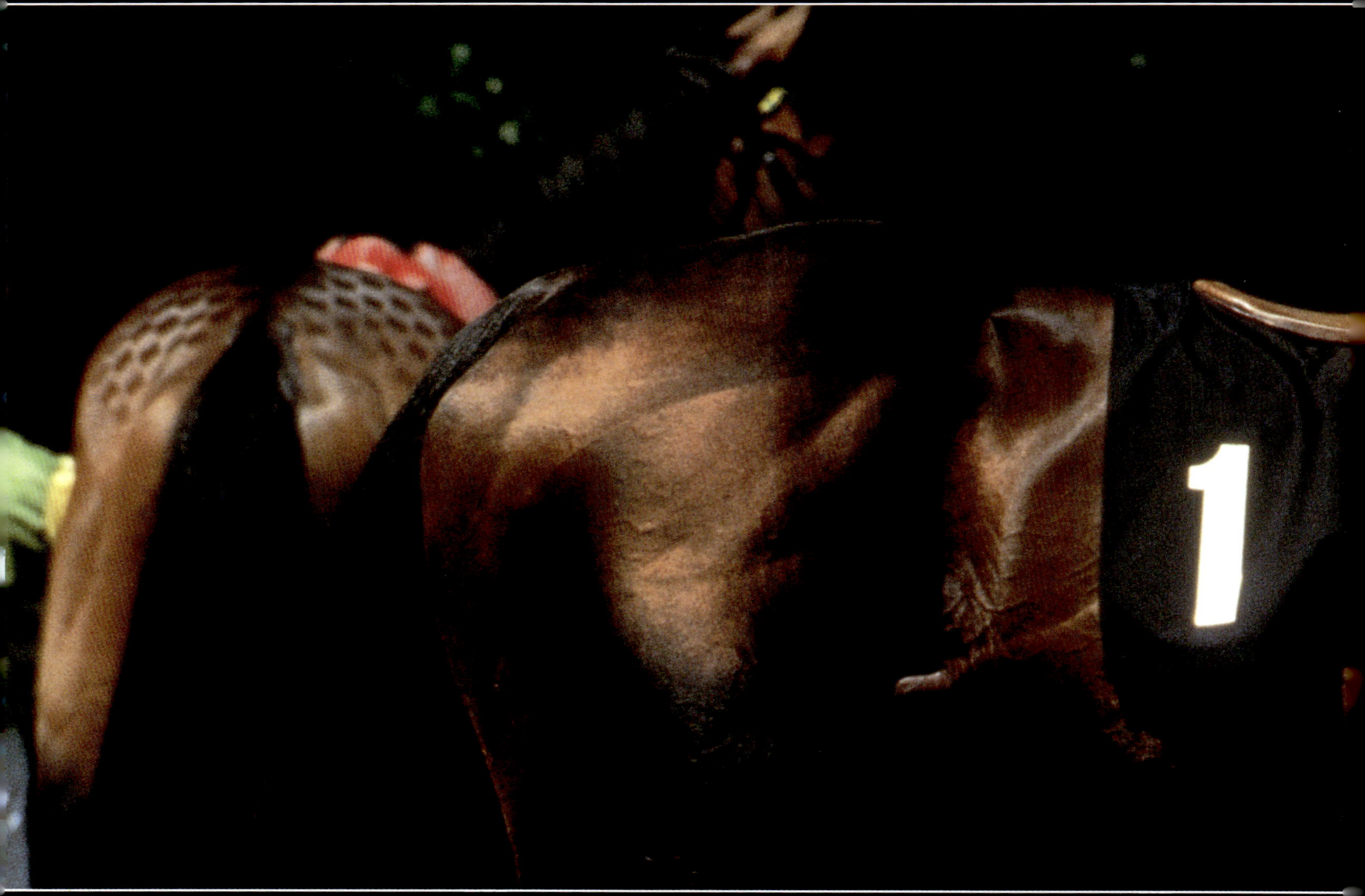
1

horses and jockeys

BASIC

The art of thoroughbred insurance

With over 20 years experience in the racing and breeding industry, we offer a range of insurance and financial services to the bloodstock investor.

For more information contact:
Hamish Scott-Dalgleish
THE BLOODSTOCK & STUD INVESTMENT COMPANY LTD.
1 THE GREEN, MARLBOROUGH, WILTS SN8 1AL
Tel: 01672 512512   Fax: 01672 516660

Thousands of horses are needed to keep the show on the road

- and most of them, sadly, do not go fast enough to earn their training fees. But the dream is kept alive by the few who do and, even more brightly, by the Stars who do much more. You never know…

Every clumsy would-be jumper might be an Arkle. Every foal you breed or buy may be worth millions after running twelve furlongs round Epsom in the June of their second season.

All thoroughbreds are descended from the same three stallions (The Byerley, Godolphin and Darley Arabians), but so-called "selective" breeding has had some queer results.

Red Rum (three Grand Nationals) was bred to be a sprinter and, as a two year old, deadheated in a five furlong dash, ironically, at Aintree.

Desert Orchid (four King George V1 Chases) lay apparently dying after a fall in his first hurdle race. And all the time, nearly every day of the year, the huge majority of 'ordinary' bit-player horses are exhausting themselves and risking life and limb for our enjoyment.

And what of the jockeys?

Most start as stable lads - glad to brave long hours and freezing mornings on the remote 'lottery' chance of becoming a Champion. They don't start as early now as Lester - who rode his first winner at the age of twelve. But he - and now I suppose, Dettori, Dunwoody and McCoy - are the targets at which they aim. 'Lester' is still the only one instantly identifiable by his Christian name.

As his career proves, jockeys come in all shapes and sizes. Lester spent 40 years nearly two stone below his 'normal' body weight. Stan Mellor (three times jump Champion) used often to carry two stone of lead and Dave Dick, who won the 1942 Lincoln on Gloaming with 7st 4lbs, carried 11st 3lbs (wasting hard for both!) when ESB won the 1956 Grand National.

A jump jockey's basic wage may be higher - £84.50 a ride against £61.50 - but they have much shorter careers, a far greater chance of injury and only a fraction of the prizemoney percentages available to the miniature millionaires of the flat. In the jump changing room, the comradeship of dangers shared abounds. Many started as amateurs - and might still ride for fun even if no one paid them.

Previous pages: Lester Piggott and Dear Doctor.
PHOTOGRAPH: ALLSPORT / CHRIS COLE.

Above: Fontwell Park.
PHOTOGRAPH: TREVOR JONES.

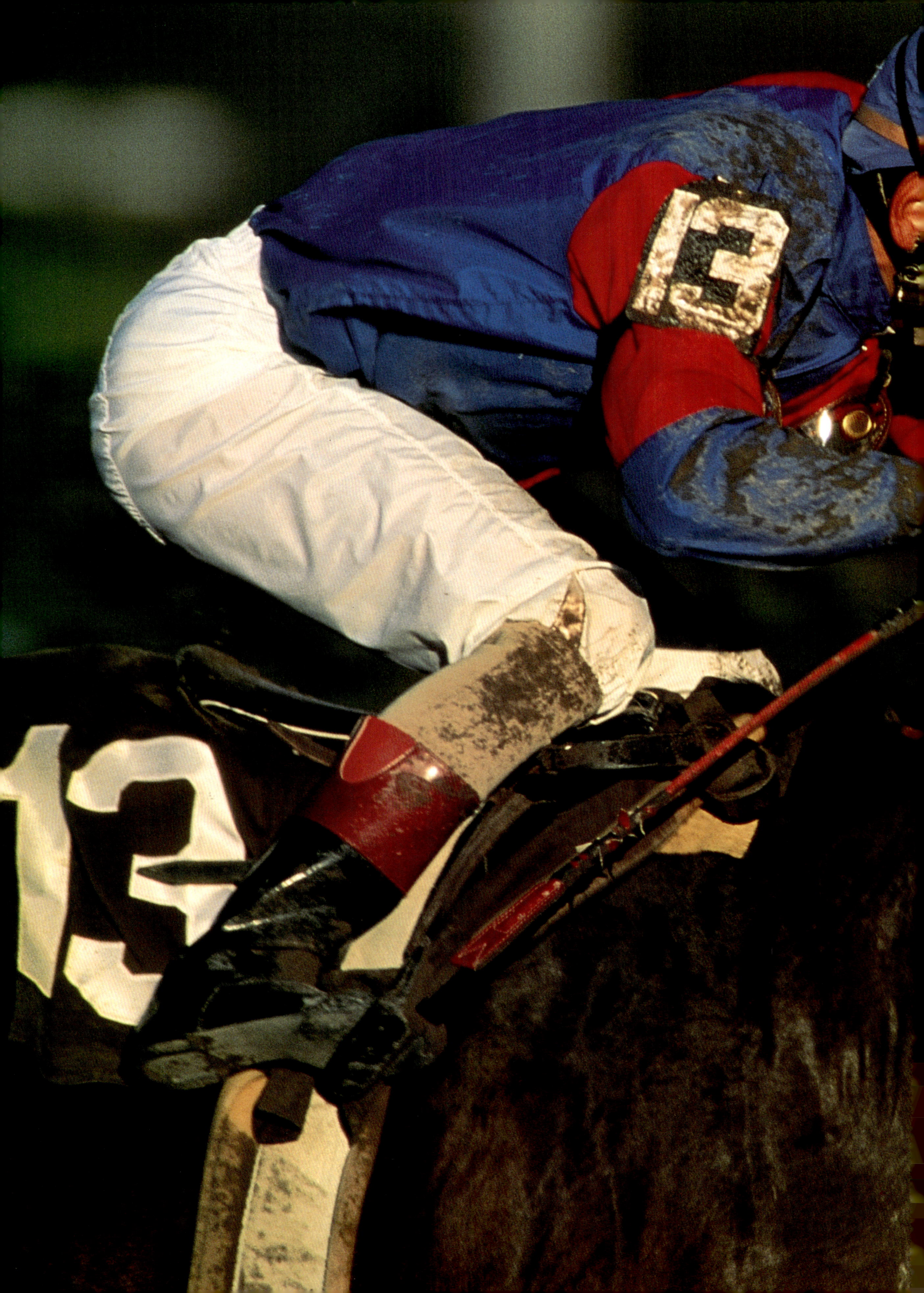

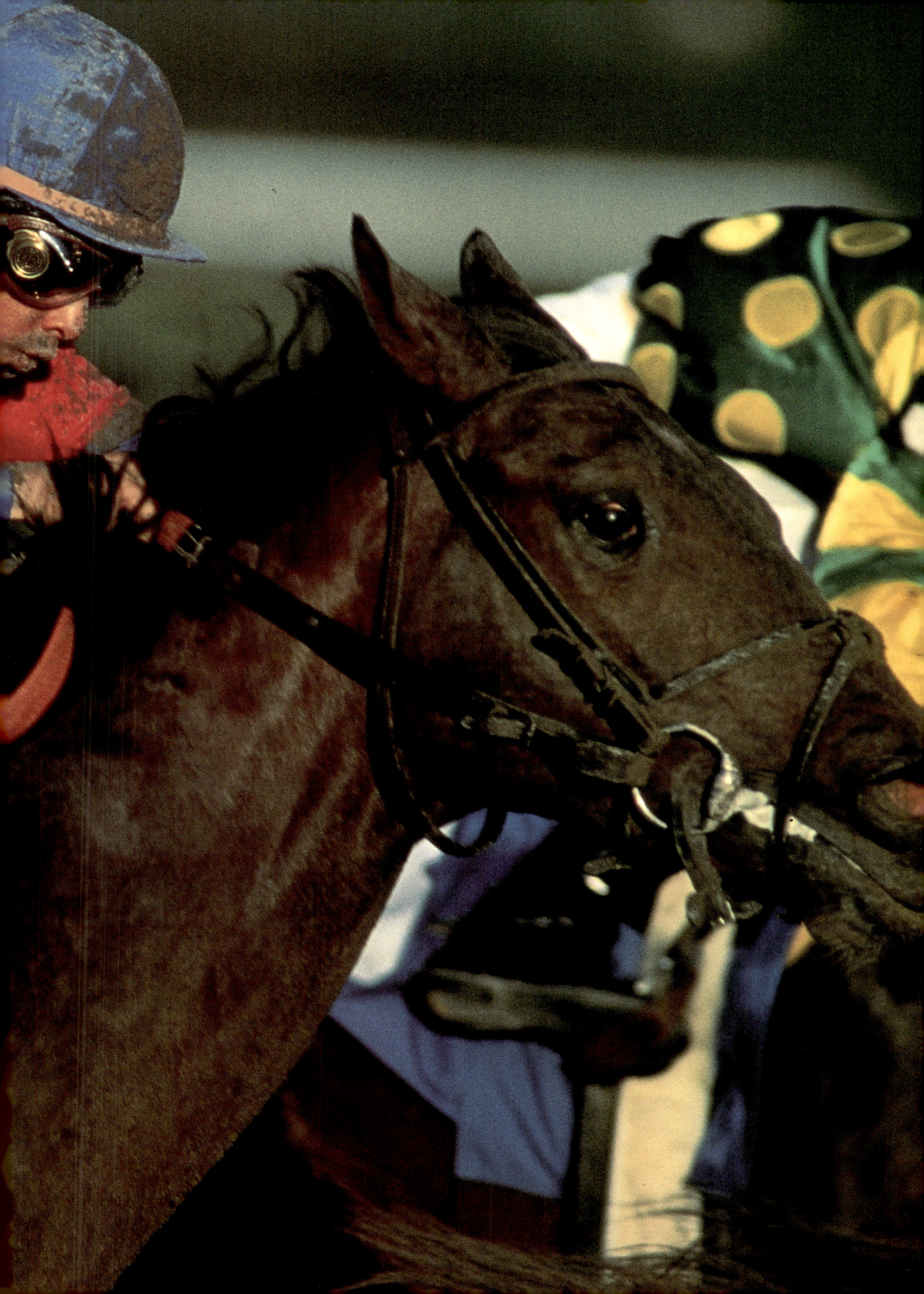

Previous pages: Total commitment.
PHOTOGRAPH: ALLSPORT / SIMON BRUTY.

Below: Jamie Osbourne studies the opposition… while Certain Style studies the fence.
PHOTOGRAPH: IAN HALL.

Right: Lester on Rodrigo de Triano before winning the 2000 Guineas.
PHOTOGRAPH: W EVERITT.

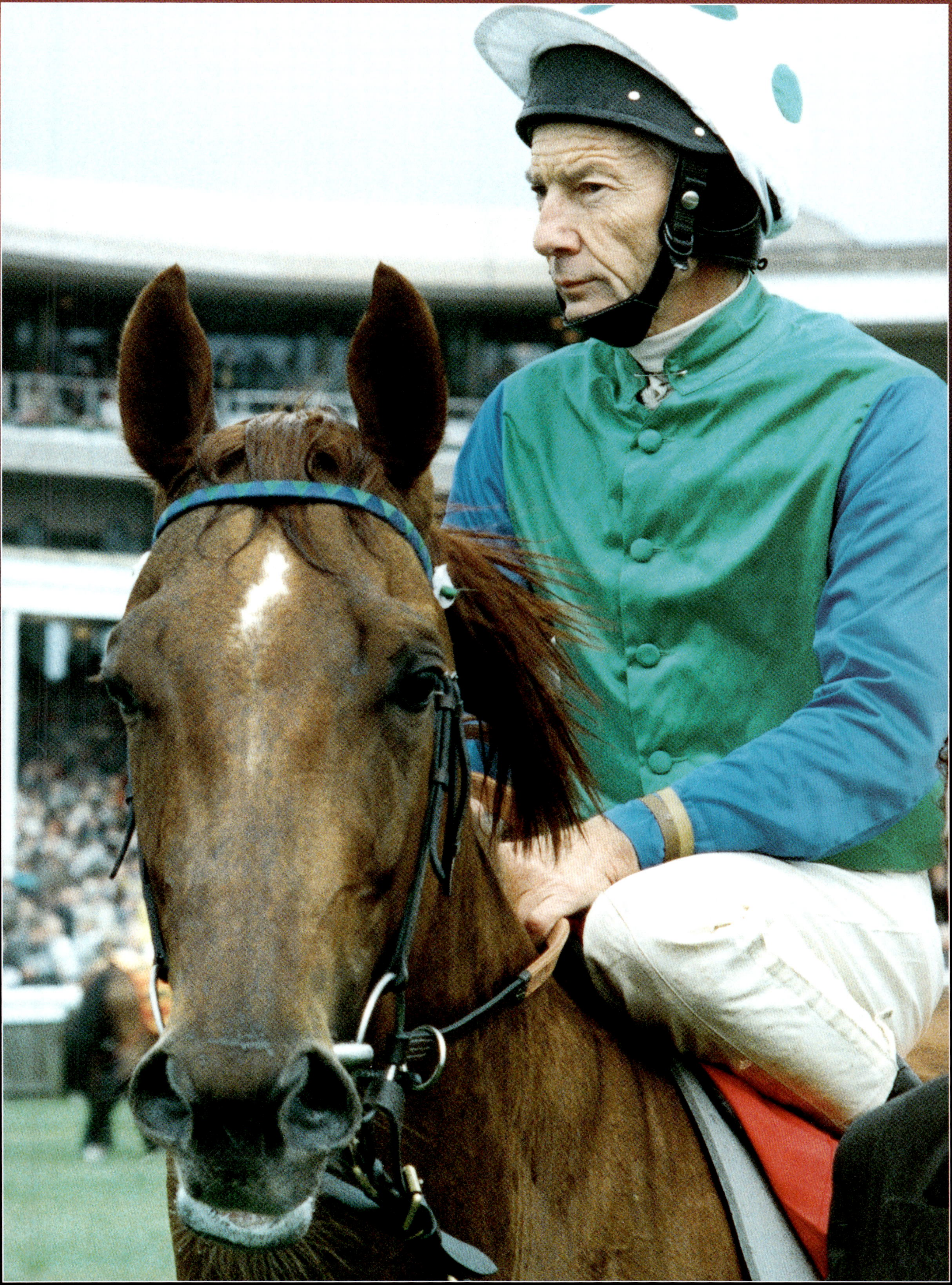

Above: Frankie practices the 'Dettori jump'.
PHOTOGRAPH: M P MALONEY.

Below: Maguire concentrates.
PHOTOGRAPH: TINA WHITE.

Above Right: Willie Carson congratulates Hamas.
PHOTOGRAPH: SPORTSPHOTO.

Below: Richard Dunwoody.
PHOTOGRAPH: TINA WHITE.

Far Right: Dirty work.
PHOTOGRAPH: TREVOR JONES.

Below Right: John Francome.
PHOTOGRAPH: TREVOR JONES.

69

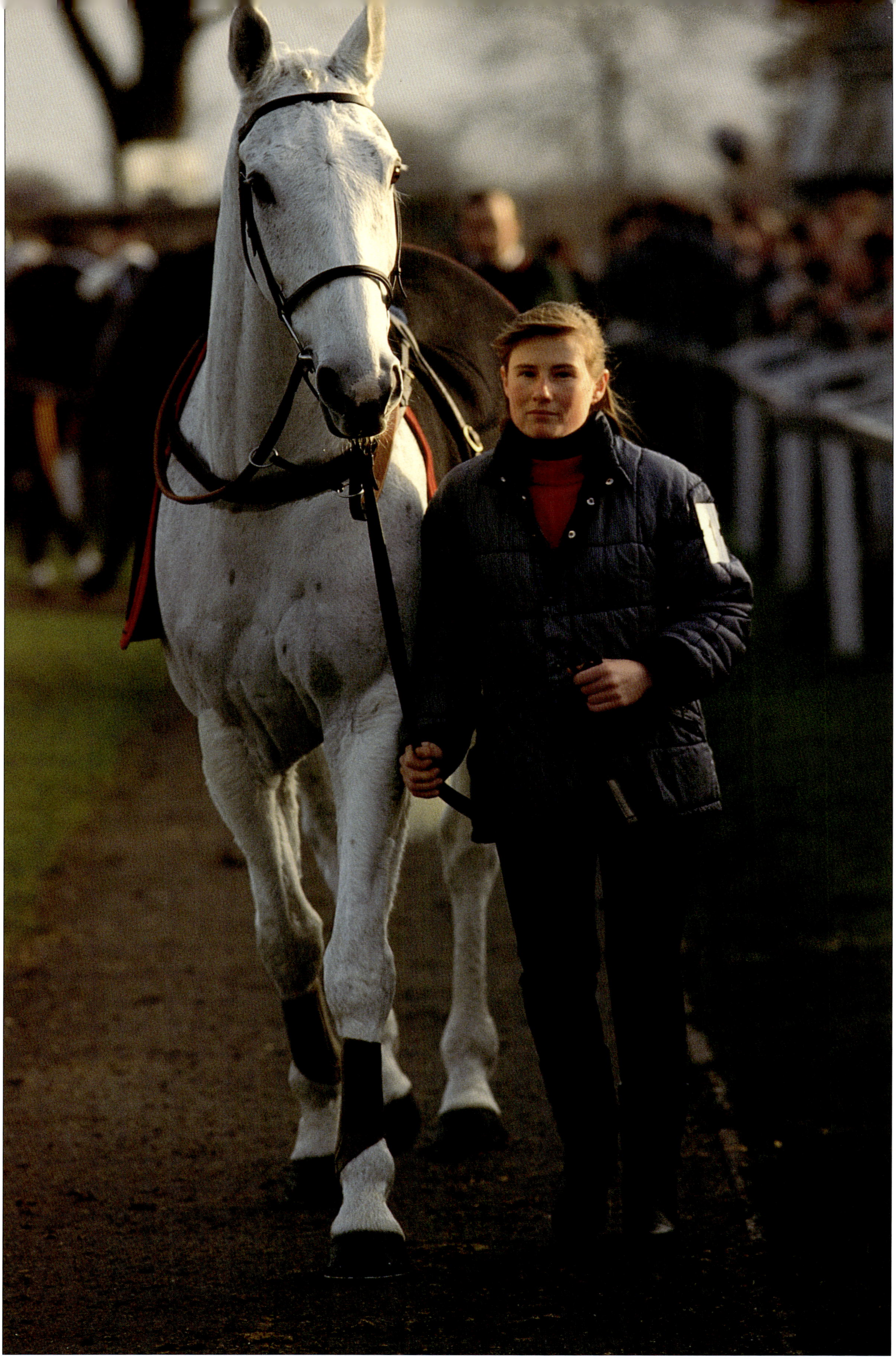

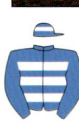

Left: A fine horse is led into the Parade Ring at Tattersalls.
PHOTOGRAPH: TREVOR JONES.

Far Left: Desert Orchid before another win.
PHOTOGRAPH: TREVOR JONES.

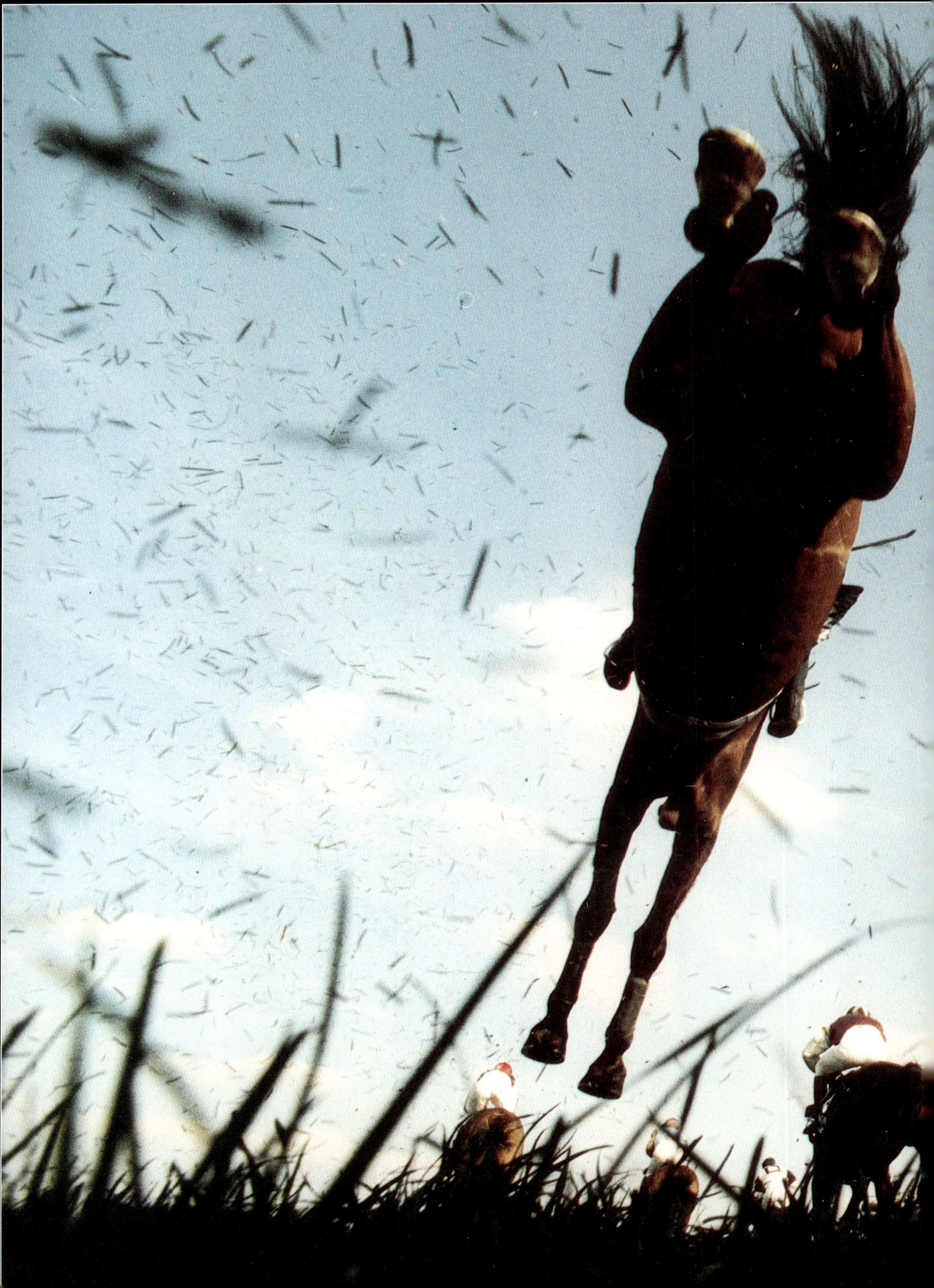

Above: 'This is easy!'
PHOTOGRAPH: SARAH REEVES.

Main photo: Airborne!
PHOTOGRAPH: M P MALONEY.
(WINNER OF THE 'HORSES' CATEGORY).

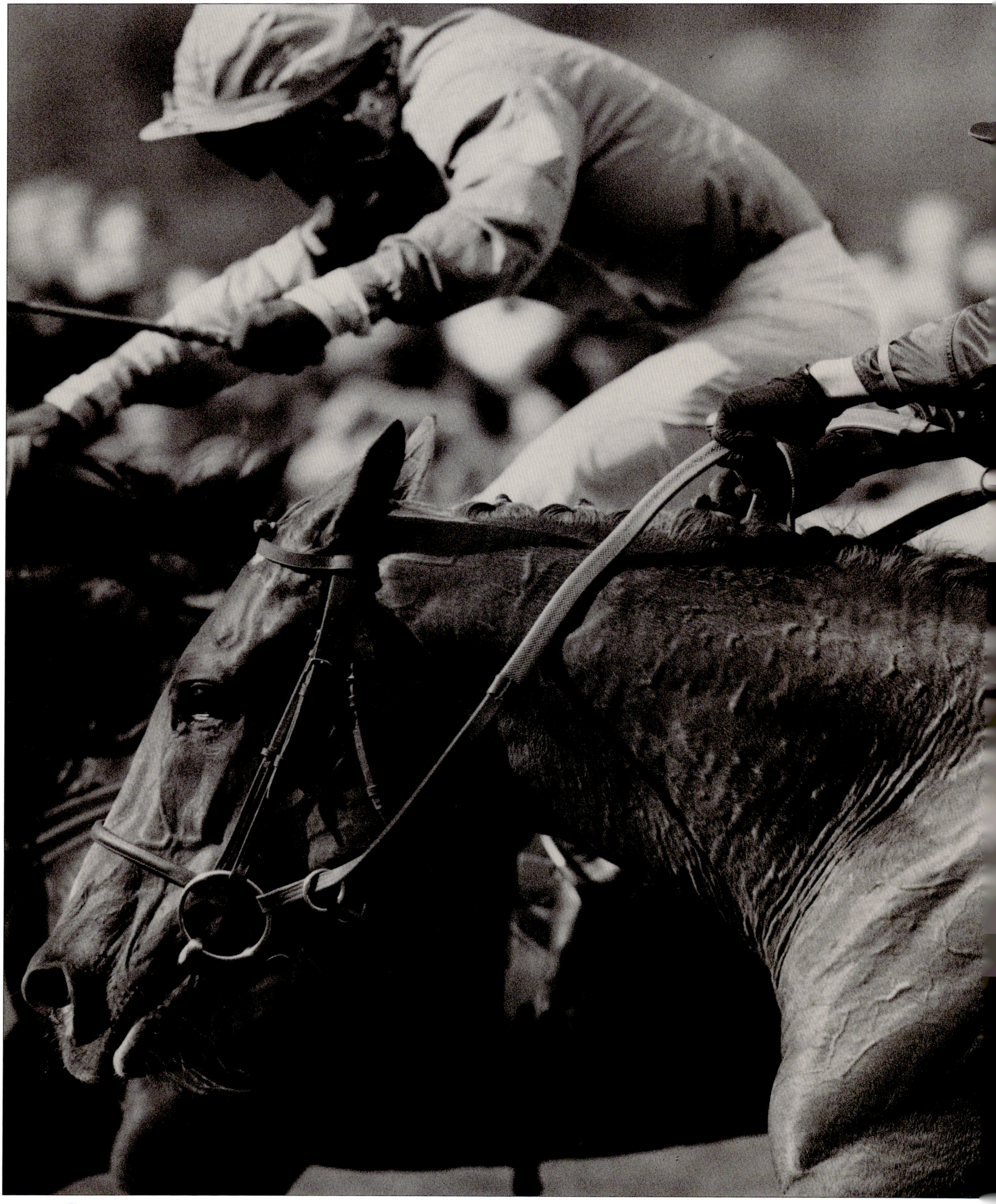

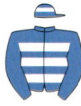

Above: G. Mosse at Deauville.
PHOTOGRAPH: TREVOR JONES.

Main Photo: A fighting finish for Fighting Words in the Whitbread Gold Cup at Sandown Park.
PHOTOGRAPH: JOHN CHASE.
(WINNER OF THE 'JOCKEYS' CATEGORY).

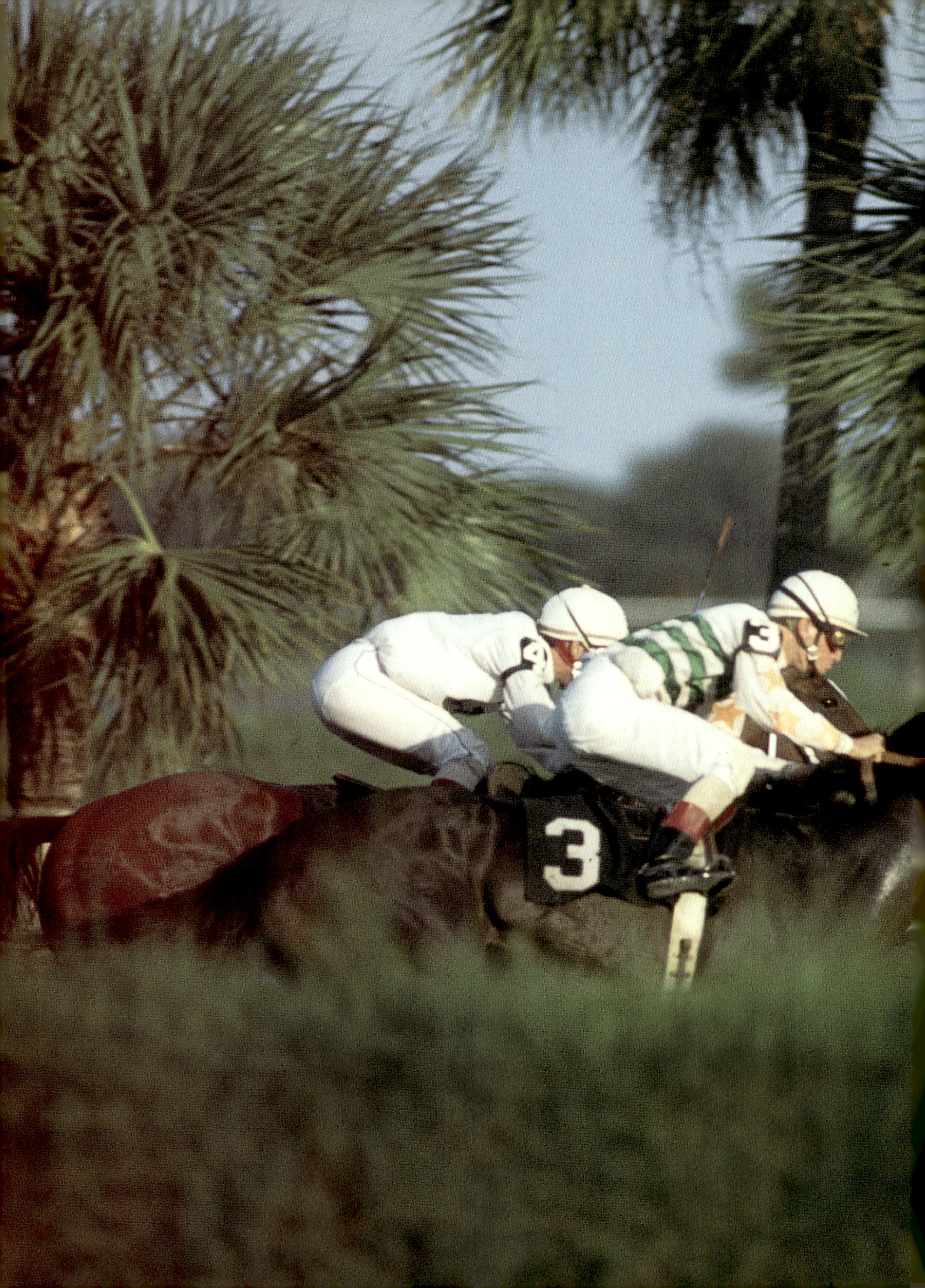
3

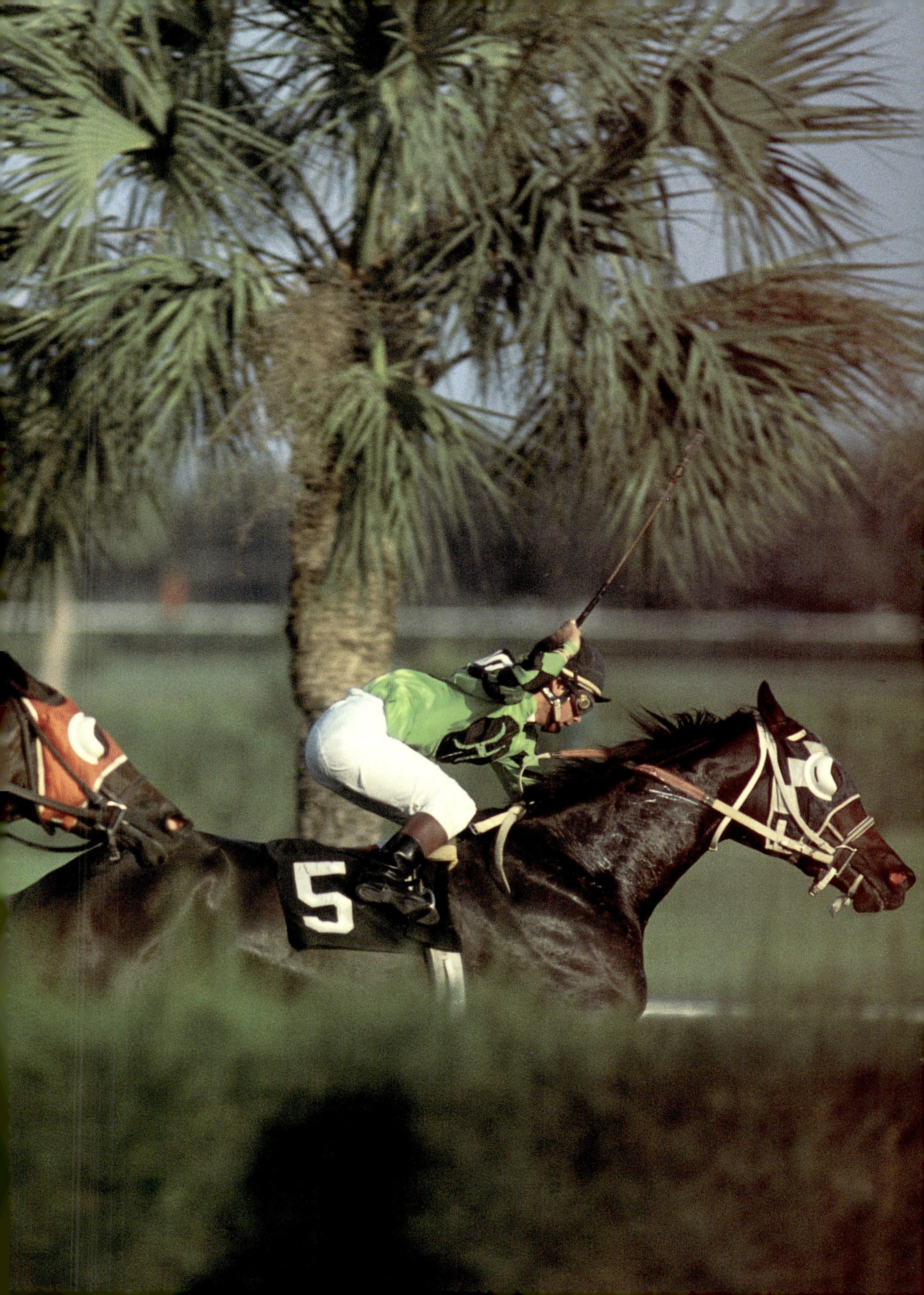
5

Previous pages: Horses and Jockeys.
PHOTOGRAPH: TREVOR JONES.

Main Photo: A fine stallion.
PHOTOGRAPH: MISS C HOOD.

Inset Above: True love.
PHOTOGRAPH: DAVID RENTON.

Inset Right: Desert Orchid in retirement.
PHOTOGRAPH: KENNETH HARGREAVES.

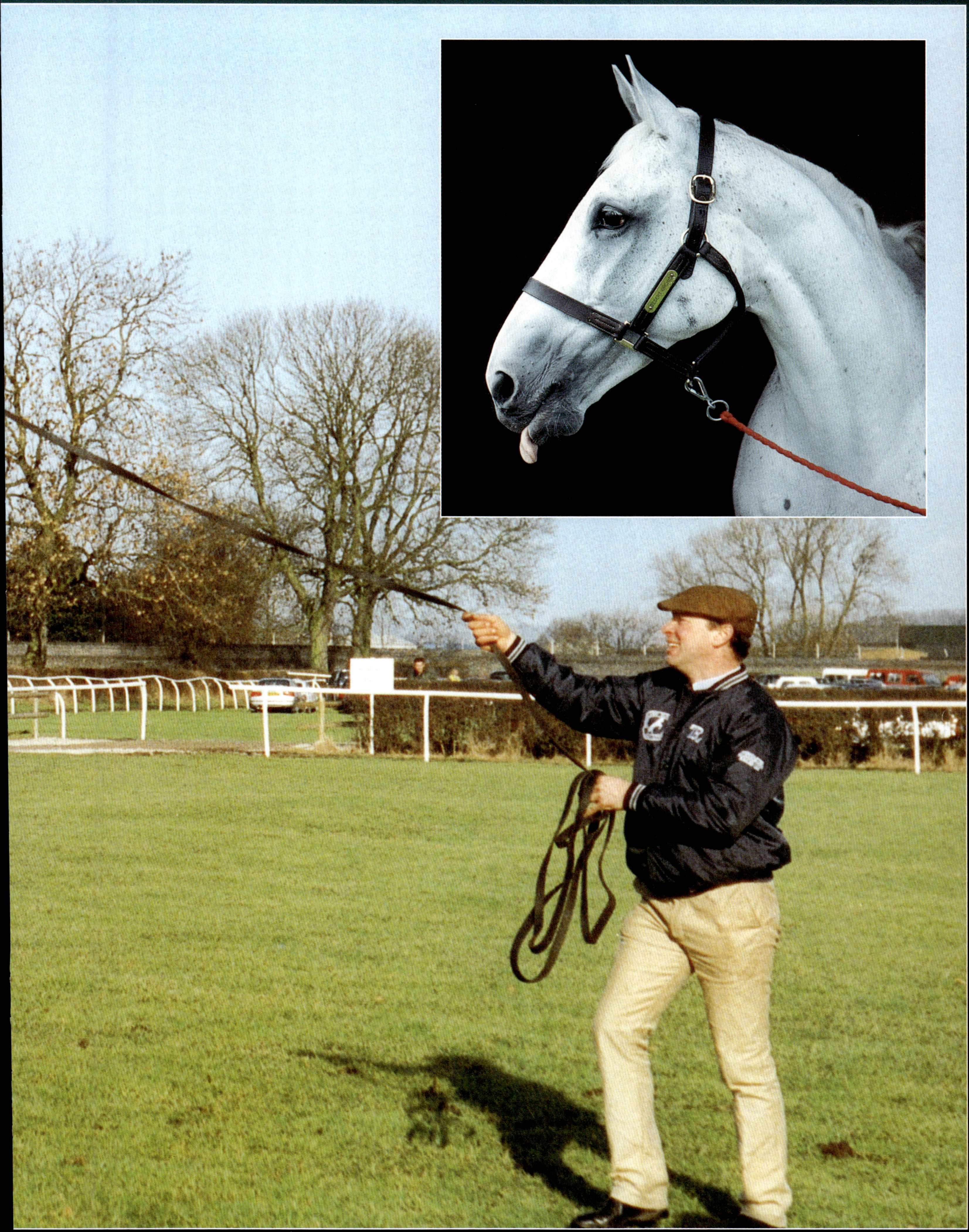

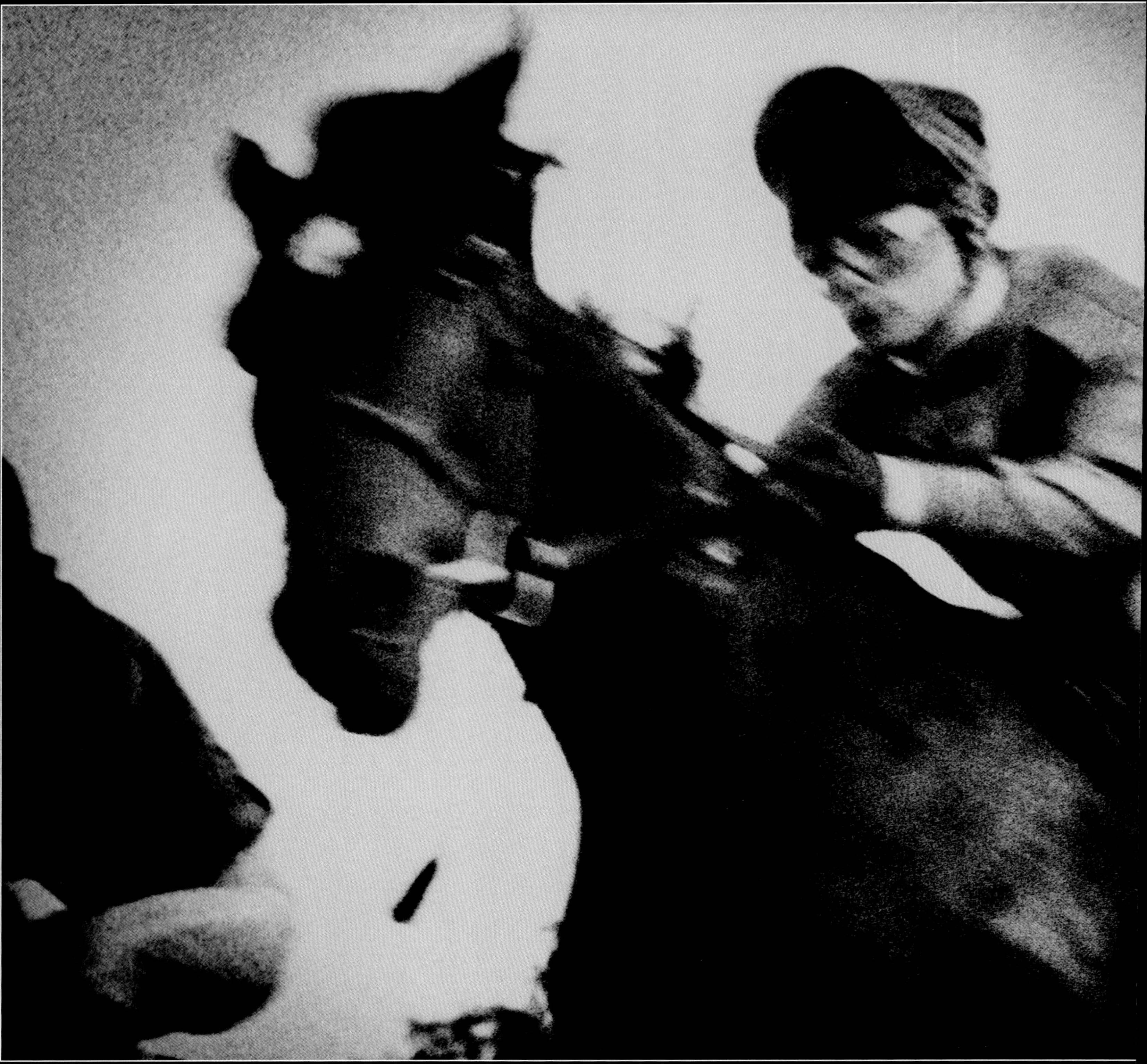

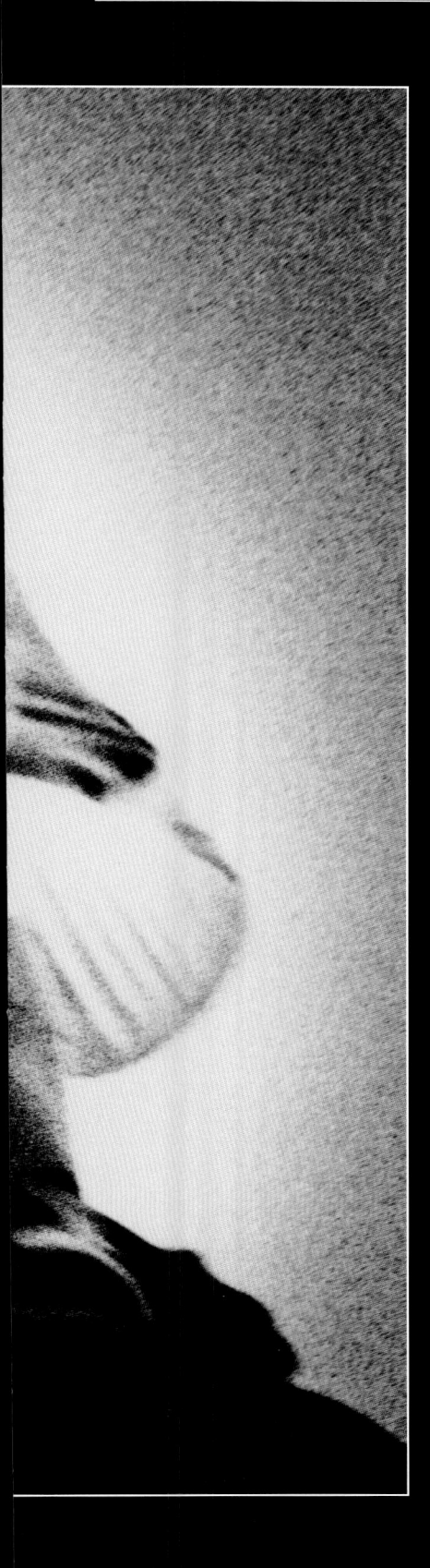

Left: A blur of speed.
PHOTOGRAPH: JOHN CHASE.

Below: It always happens in front of the camera!
PHOTOGRAPH: STEPHEN BENNETT.

Next Page: The runners return.
PHOTOGRAPH: TREVOR JONES.

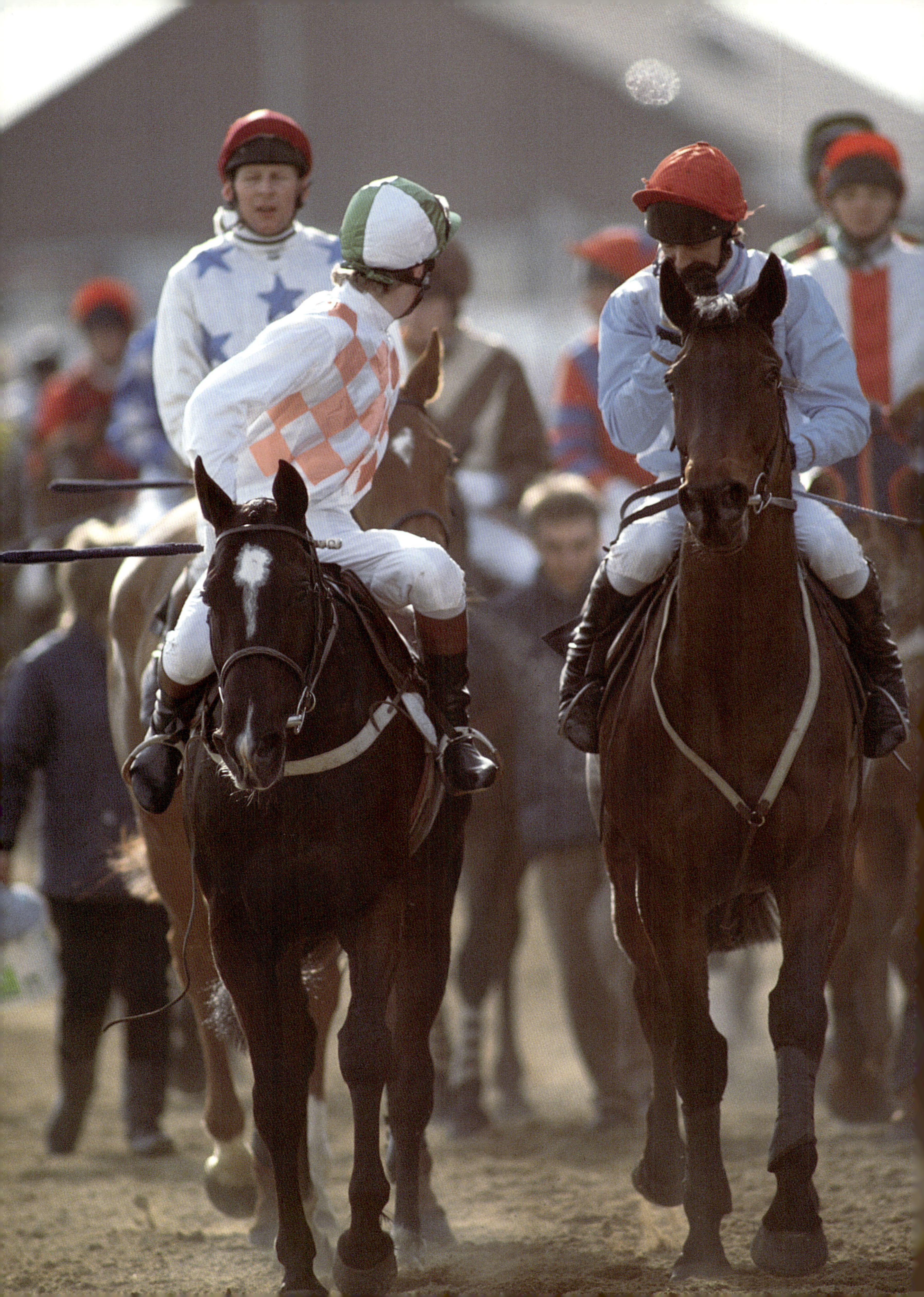

The Cadogan Group – a business with breadth

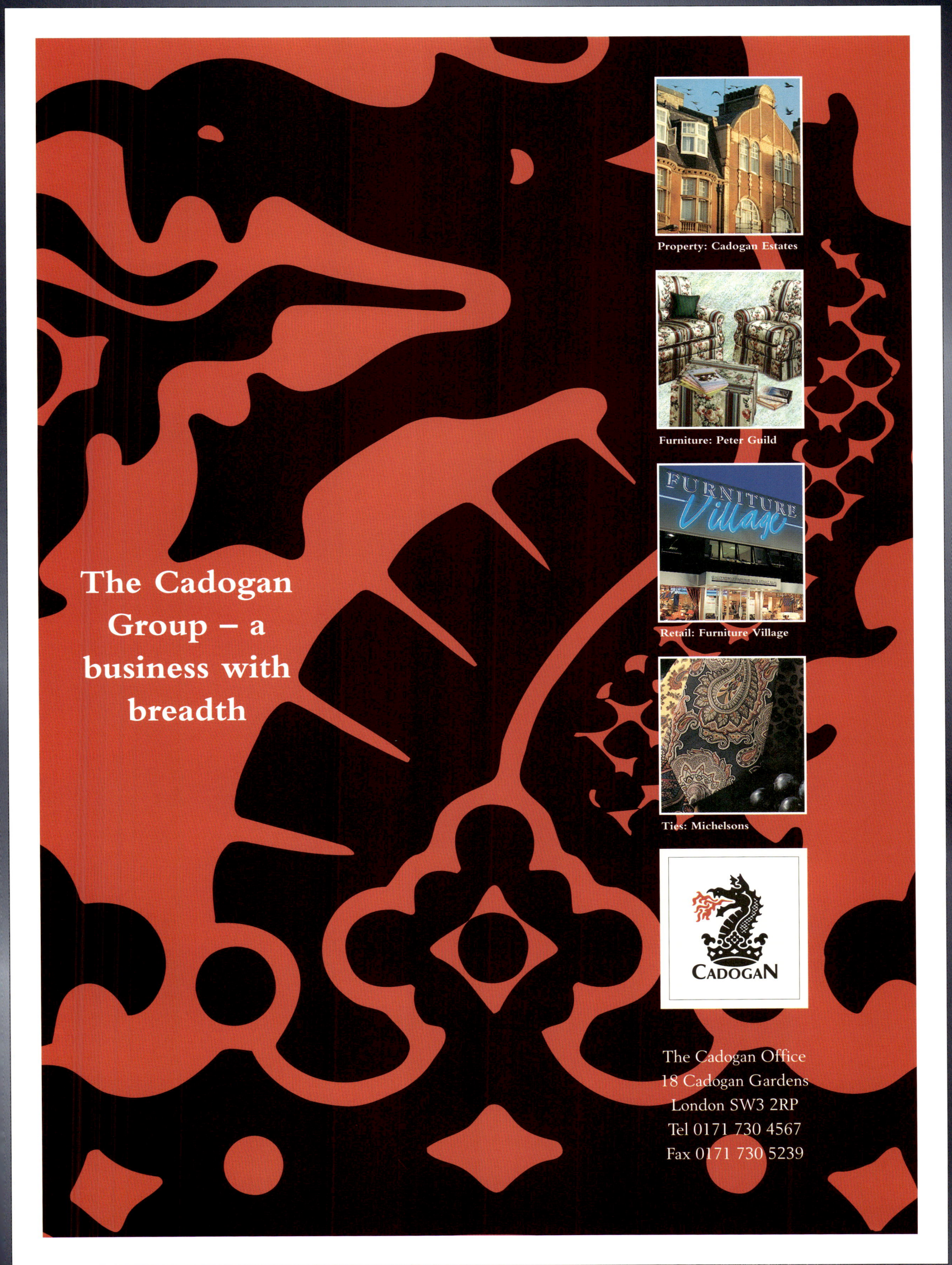

Property: Cadogan Estates

Furniture: Peter Guild

Retail: Furniture Village

Ties: Michelsons

CADOGAN

The Cadogan Office
18 Cadogan Gardens
London SW3 2RP
Tel 0171 730 4567
Fax 0171 730 5239

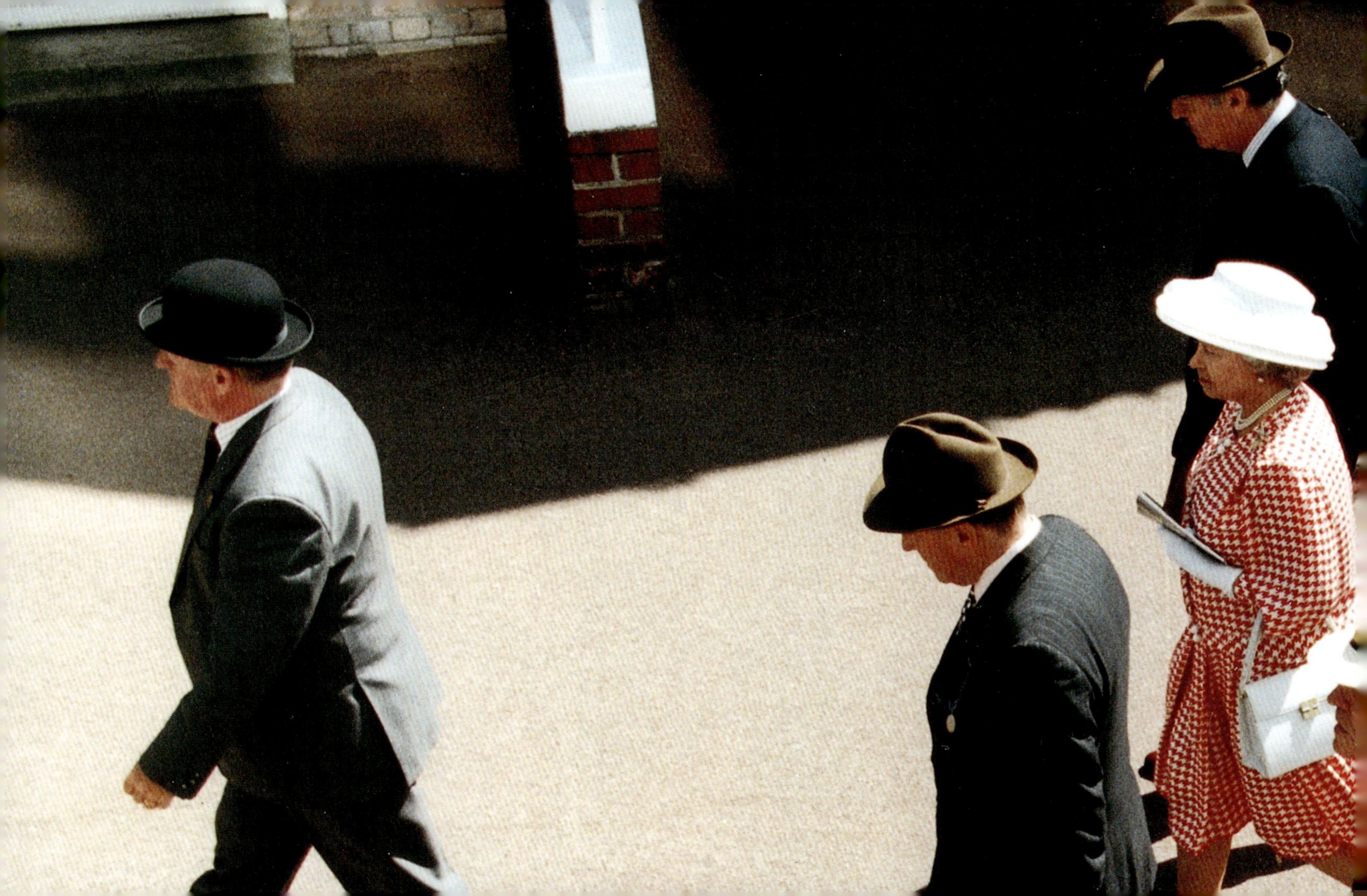

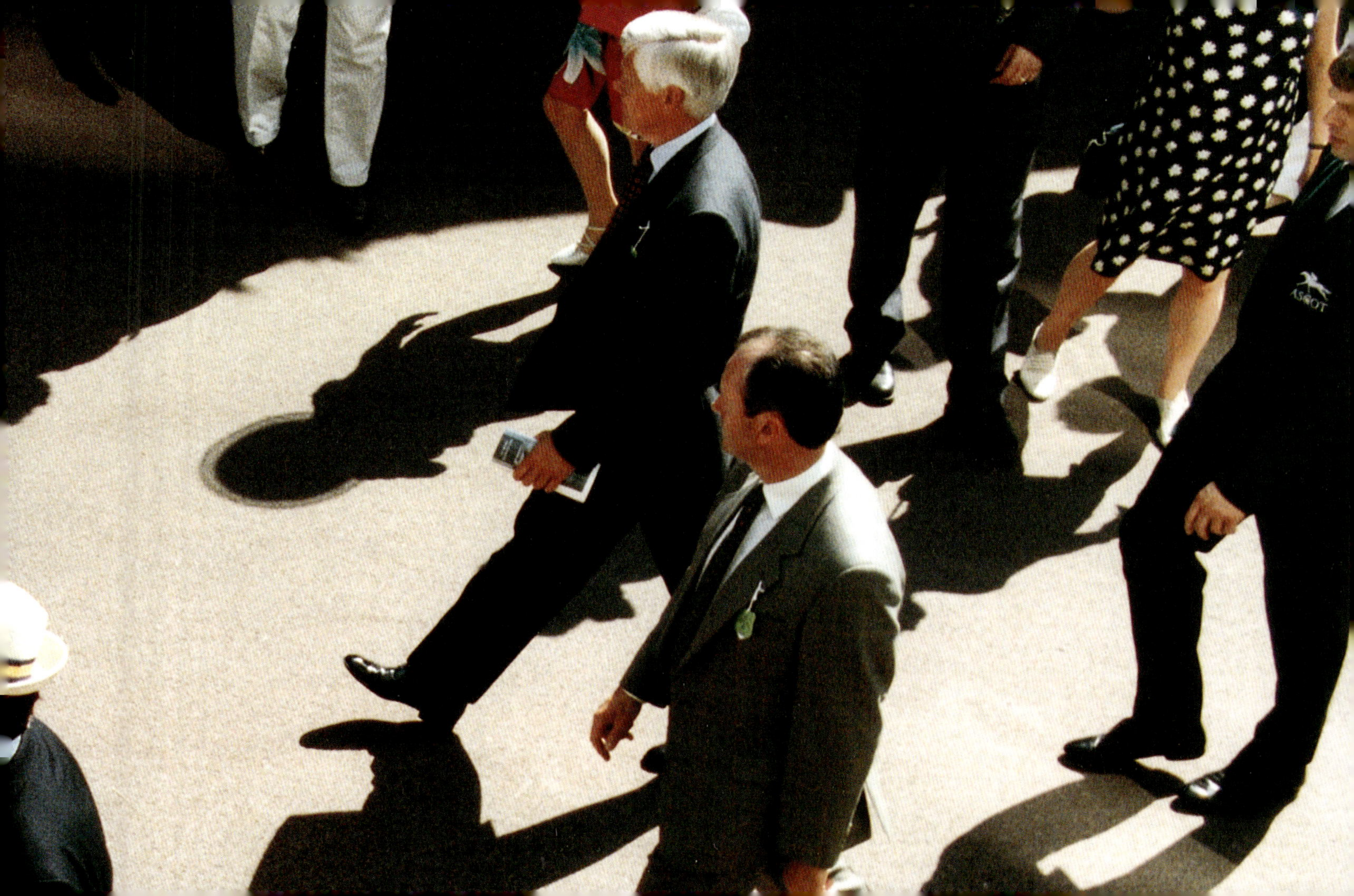
ASCOT

The Japan Racing Association

Head Office:
4-3-1 Toranomon, Minato-ku, Tokyo 105, JAPAN
Tel: 81-3-3591-5251 Fax: 81-3-3438-4893

New York Representative Office:
599 West Putnam Avenue, Greenwich, CT 06830, USA
Tel: 1-203-861-0271 Fax: 1-203-861-0272

Sydney Representative Office:
Level 38, The Chifley Tower, Sydney, AUSTRALIA
Tel: 61-2-9231-3033 Fax: 61-2-9231-3210

London Representative Office:
27 Dover Street, London W1, U.K.
Tel: 44-171-495-4333 Fax: 44-171-495-8962

Paris Representative Office:
21 Boulevard de la Madeleine, 75038 Paris, FRANCE
Tel: 33-1-47-03-94-50 Fax: 33-1-47-03-94-60

Hong Kong Representative Office:
1510 Two Pacific Place, 88 Queensway, HONG KONG
Tel: 852-2840-1566 Fax: 852-2840-1397

"On the Turf and under it, all men are equal."

A slight exaggeration perhaps - but anyone taking an across-the-board sample from a Royal Ascot or Cheltenham crowd would not find many types or classes unrepresented.

Of course those are the big occasions. Most weekday crowds are far smaller and even at weekends it is only a big race like the Whitbread, Eclipse or King George - or the presence of a real equine star like Desert Orchid - which really fills the stands.

What brings them? For many, no question, it is the gambling - tax-free on course these days which ought to make the racecourse so much more attractive than a betting shop.

But for many the horses still come first. In Britain, unlike most other major racing nations, the Parade Ring is an area of vital importance. Spectators really want to *see* their heroes. For the true horse lover, the finishing order is far less important than that they come back safe.

Previous pages: All the Queen's men.
PHOTOGRAPH: M P MALONEY.

Right: The Parade Ring at York.
PHOTOGRAPH: TREVOR JONES.

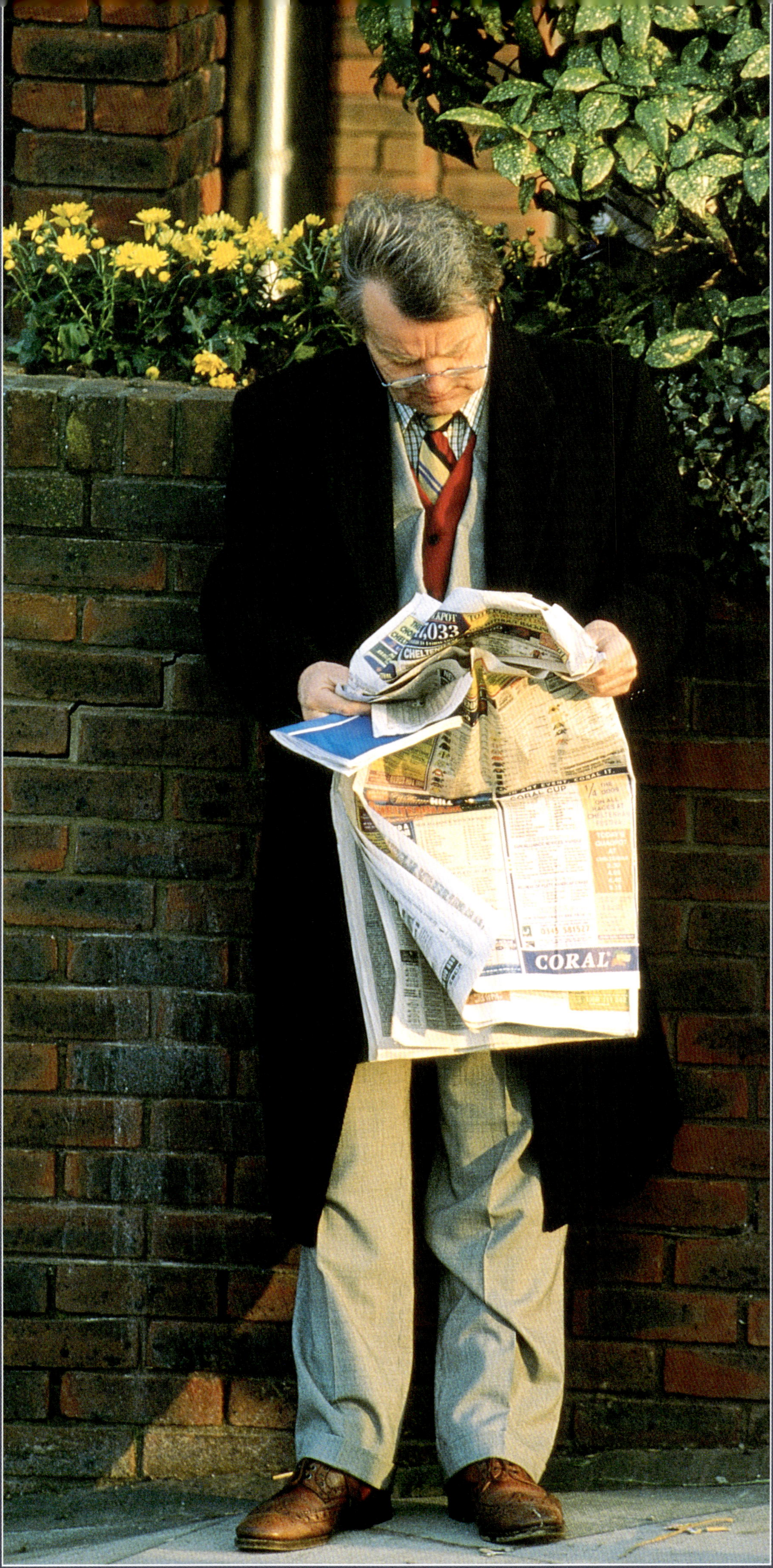
CORAL

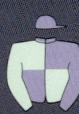

Studying the form.
PHOTOGRAPH ABOVE: ALLSPORT.
PHOTOGRAPHS LEFT AND BELOW: ALLSPORT / STU FORSTER.

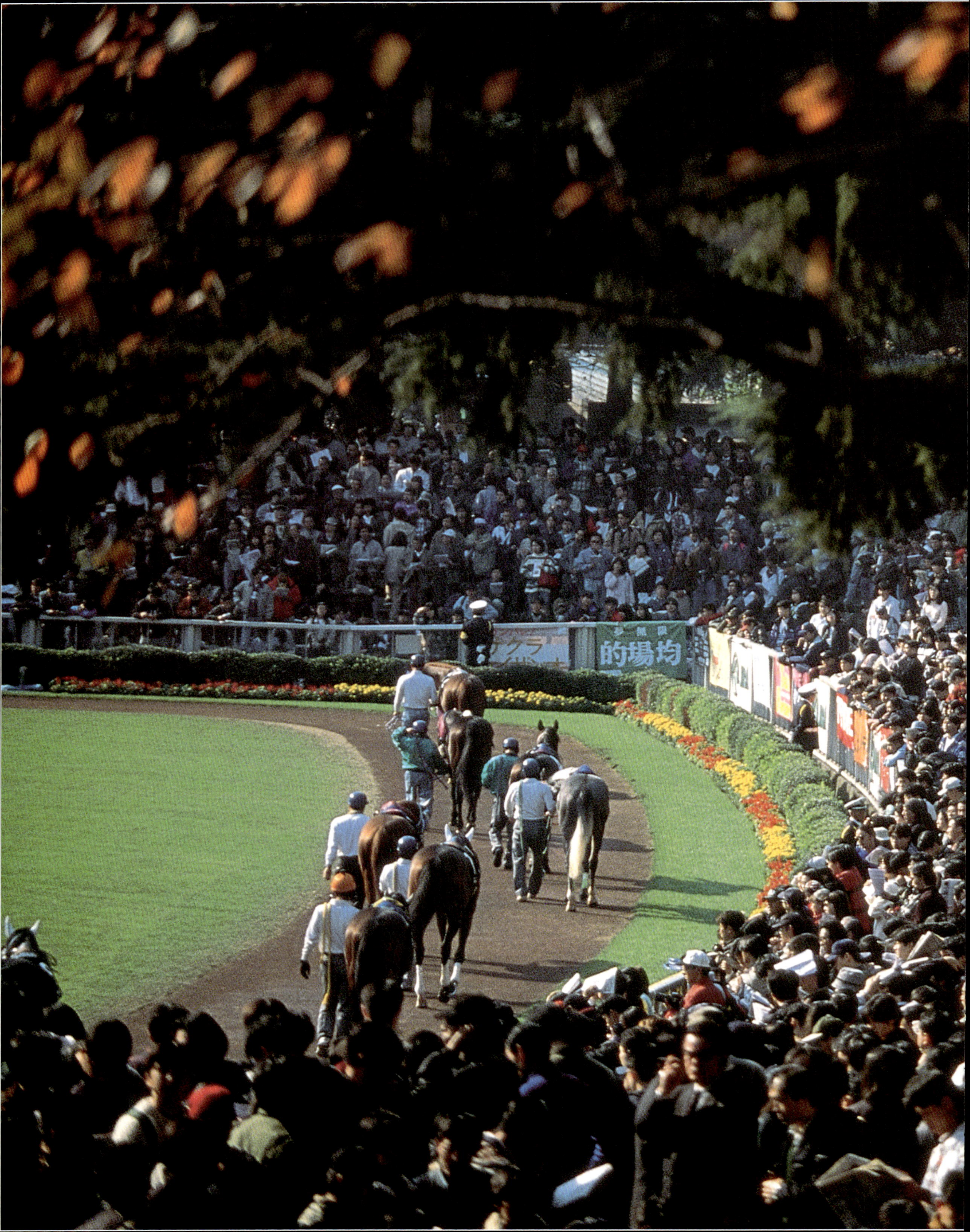
的場均

The Parade Ring at Tokyo racecourse.
PHOTOGRAPH: ALLSPORT / ANTON WANT.

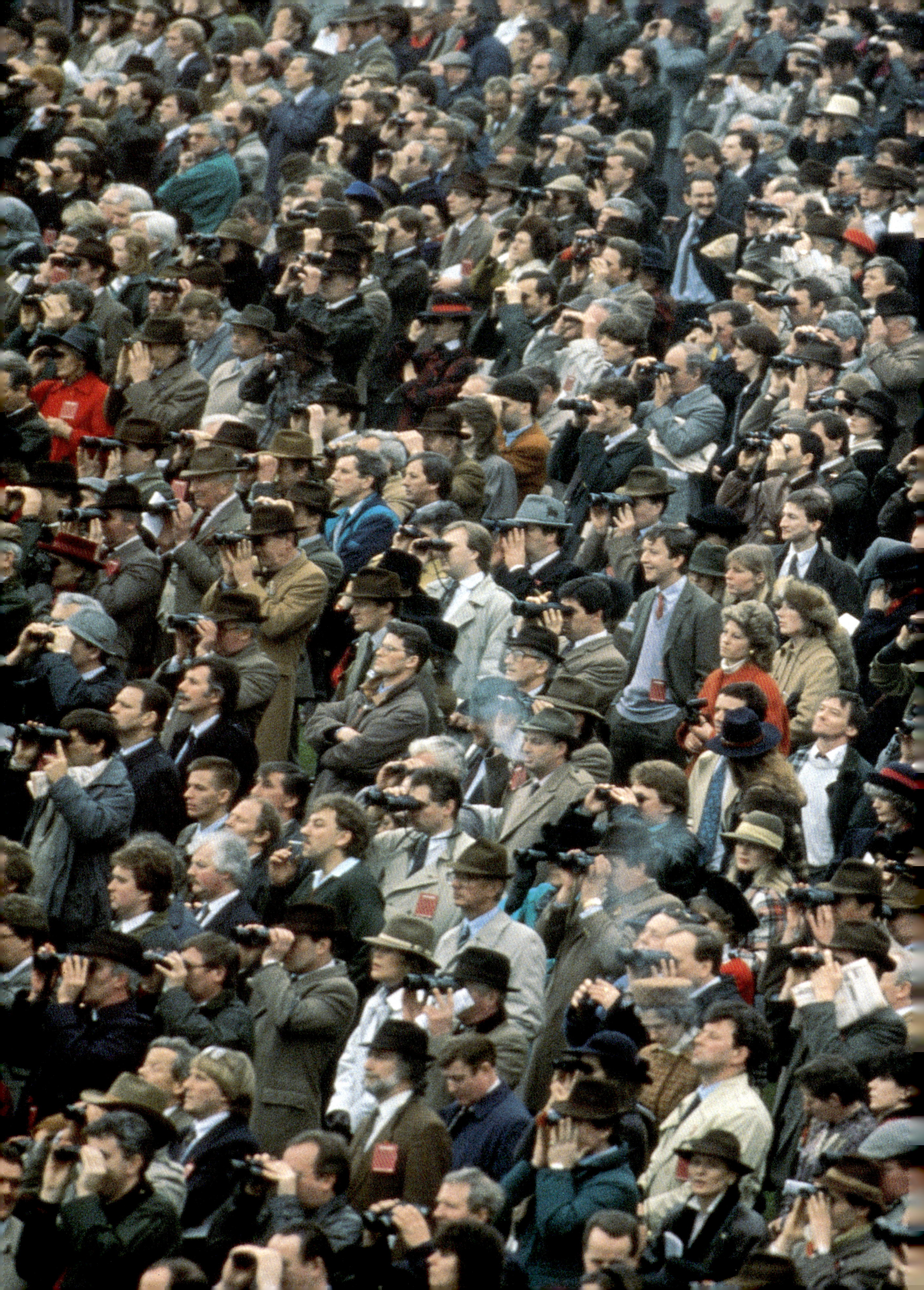

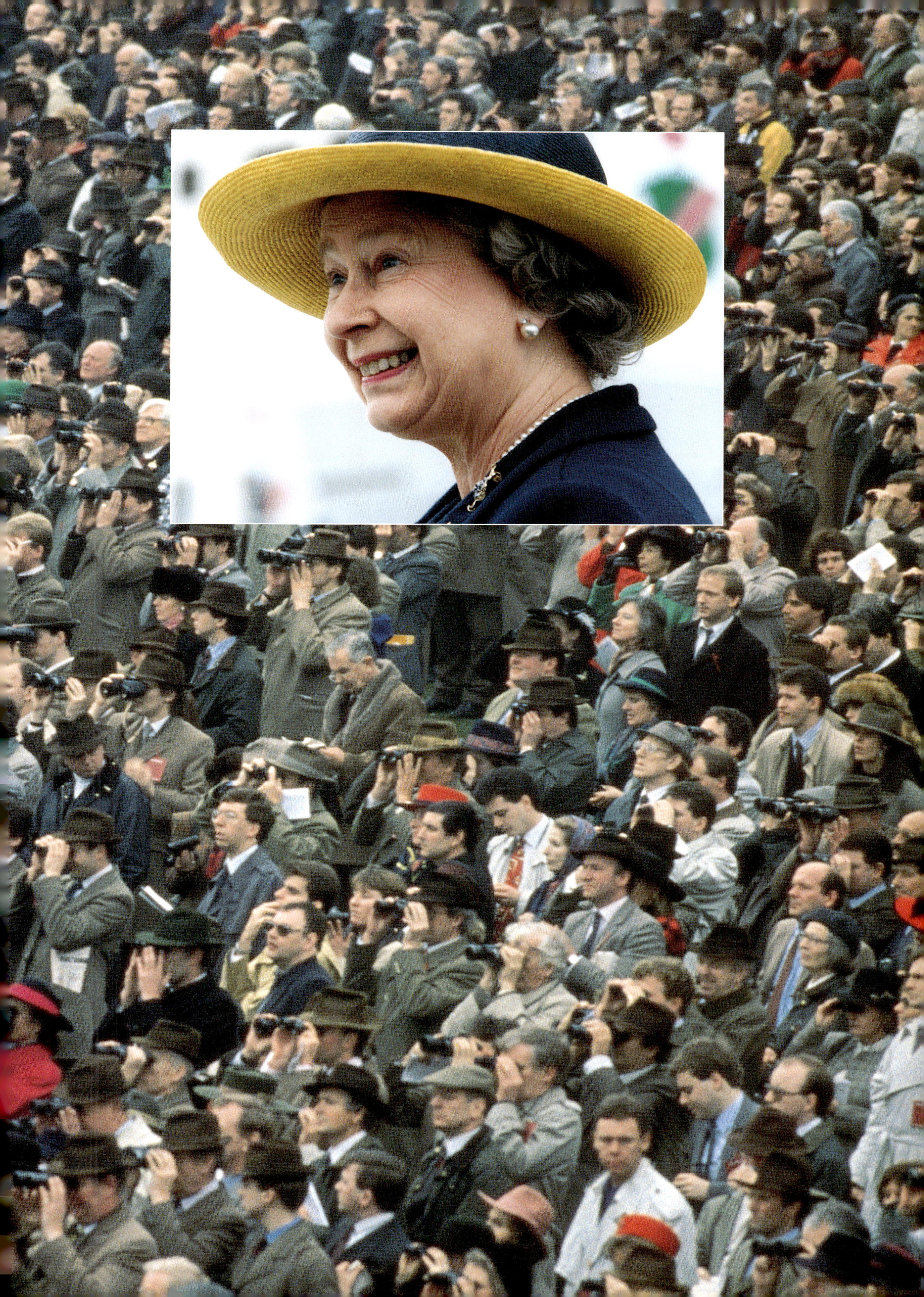

Previous pages, main picture: Packed crowds at Cheltenham.
PHOTOGRAPH: ALLSPORT / SIMON BRUTY.

Previous pages, inset: 'I think I've won!'
PHOTOGRAPH: TINA WHITE.

These pages: Ladies at Ascot.
PHOTOGRAPHS ABOVE, TOP LEFT AND RIGHT:
ALLSPORT / CHRIS COLE.
TOP CENTRE AND LEFT: ALLSPORT / MIKE HEWITT.
TOP FAR RIGHT: ALLSPORT / STU FORSTER.
BOTTOM FAR RIGHT: ALLSPORT / PASCAL RONDEAU.

95

Spectators.
PHOTOGRAPH ABOVE: TREVOR JONES.
MAIN PHOTOGRAPH: COURTESY UNITED RACECOURSES.

97

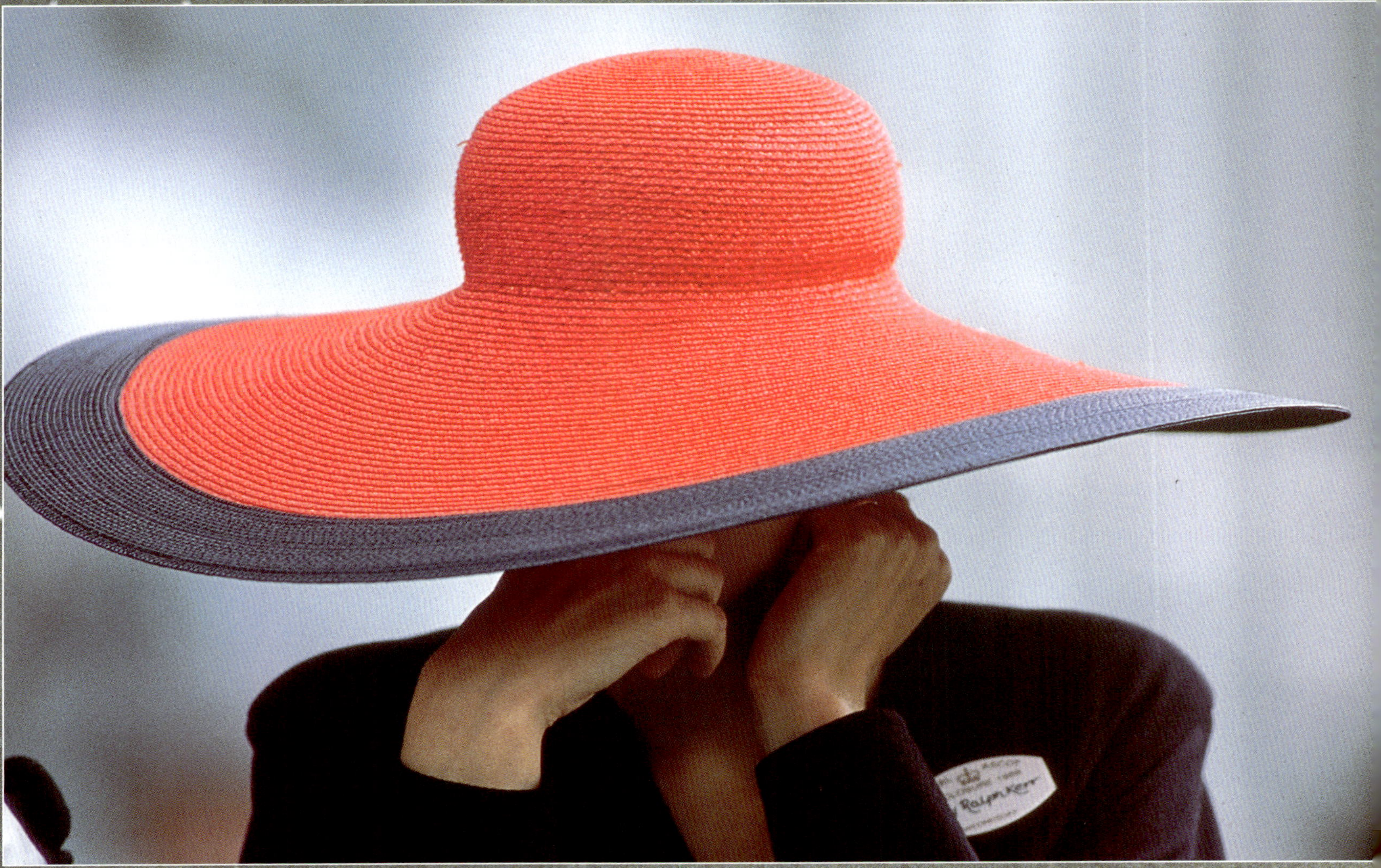

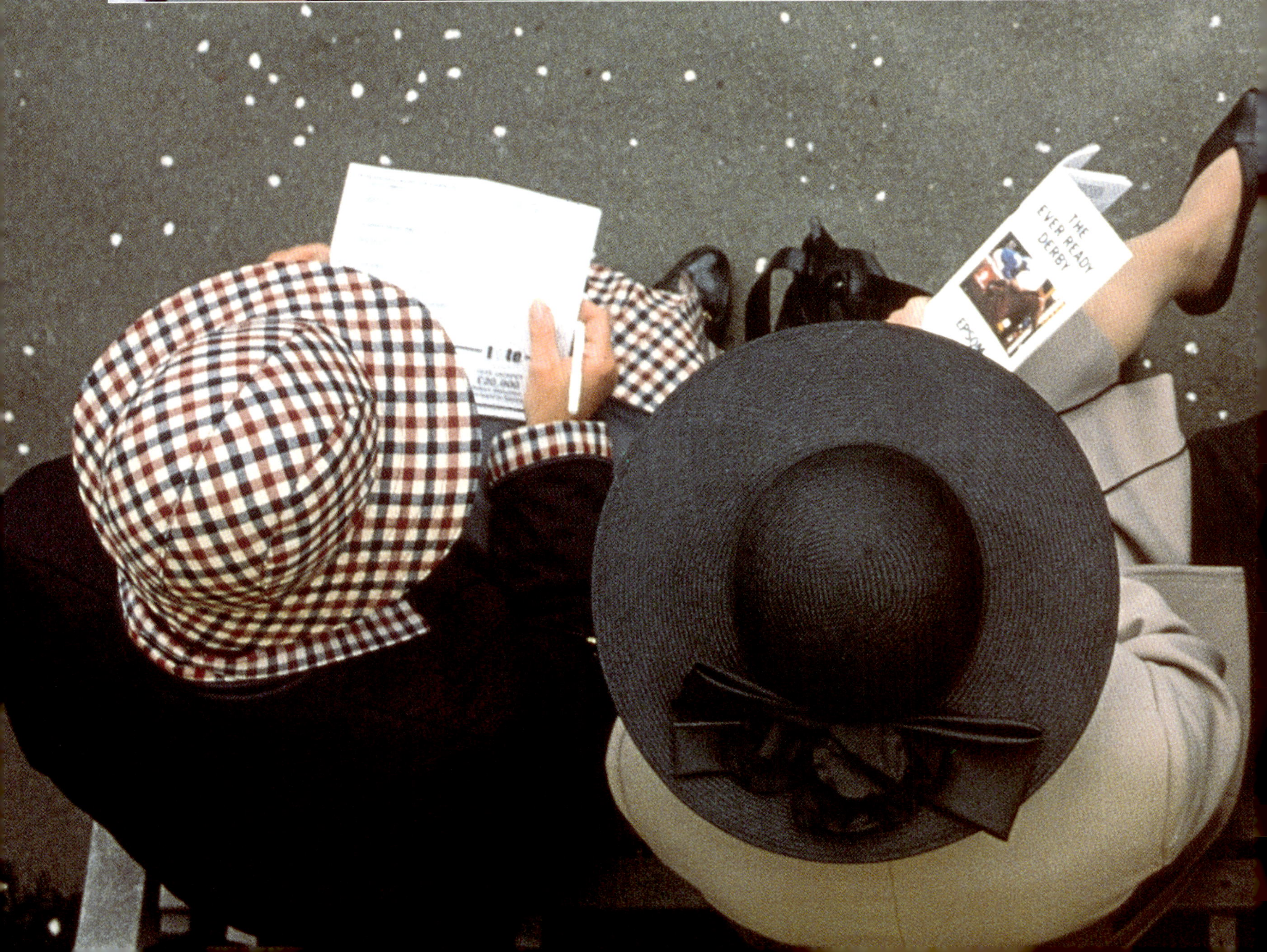
THE
EVER READY
DERBY
EPSOM

Hats.
PHOTOGRAPHS: ALLSPORT / SIMON BRUTY.

Inset: Different priorities!
PHOTOGRAPH: ALLSPORT /
SIMON BRUTY.

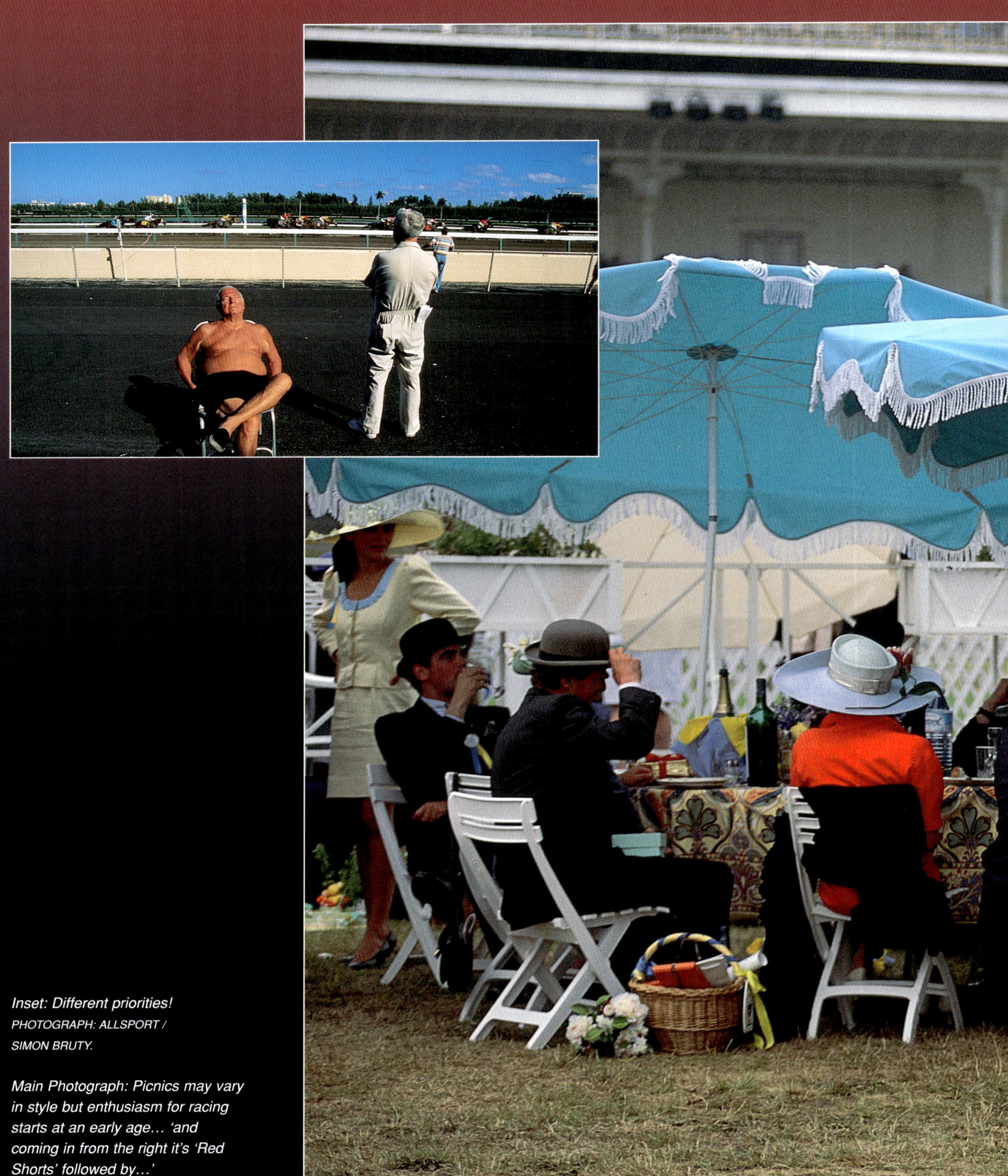

Main Photograph: Picnics may vary in style but enthusiasm for racing starts at an early age... 'and coming in from the right it's 'Red Shorts' followed by...'
PHOTOGRAPH: TREVOR JONES.

101

102

Above: Going out for the Champion Hurdle.
PHOTOGRAPH: SARAH REEVES.
(WINNER OF THE CHAPTER CATEGORY).

Right: Studying the form.
PHOTOGRAPH: ALLSPORT / STU FORSTER.

103

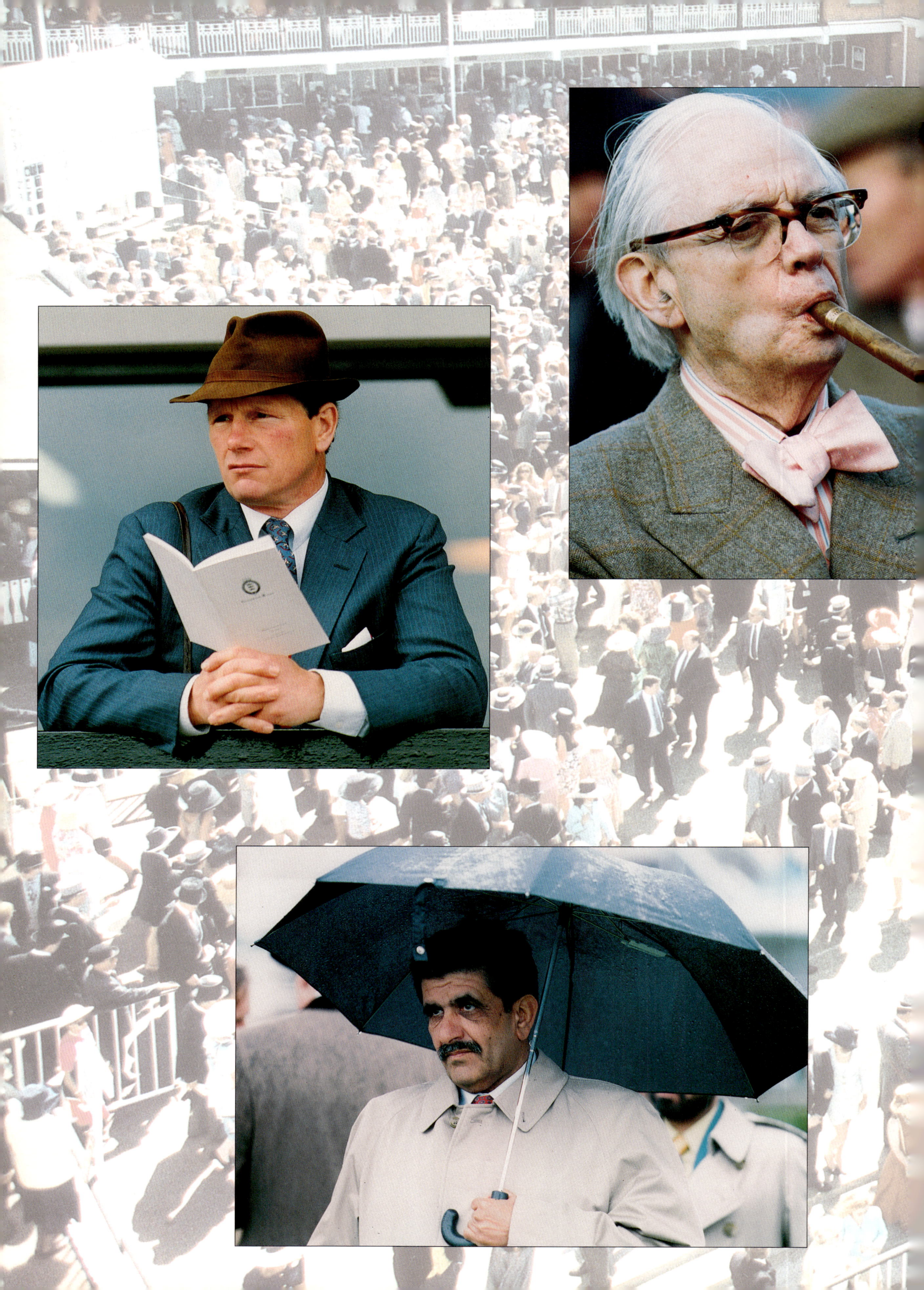

Background Photo: Royal Ascot.
PHOTOGRAPH: SPORTSPHOTO.

Above: Her Royal Highness the Queen Mother attends the Derby.
PHOTOGRAPH: M P MALONEY.

Left: I've blown it - John McCririck.
PHOTOGRAPH: SPORTSPHOTO.

Far Left: A leading trainer, Ian Balding, contemplates.
PHOTOGRAPH: SPORTSPHOTO.

Middle Top: Lord Wyatt, Chairman of the Tote for 20 years.
PHOTOGRAPH: SPORTSPHOTO.

Far Left Bottom: A leading owner, Hamdan Al-Maktoum, on a wet raceday.
PHOTOGRAPH: SPORTSPHOTO.

Many spectators like to dress for the occasion.
ALL PHOTOGRAPHS: ALLSPORT.

107

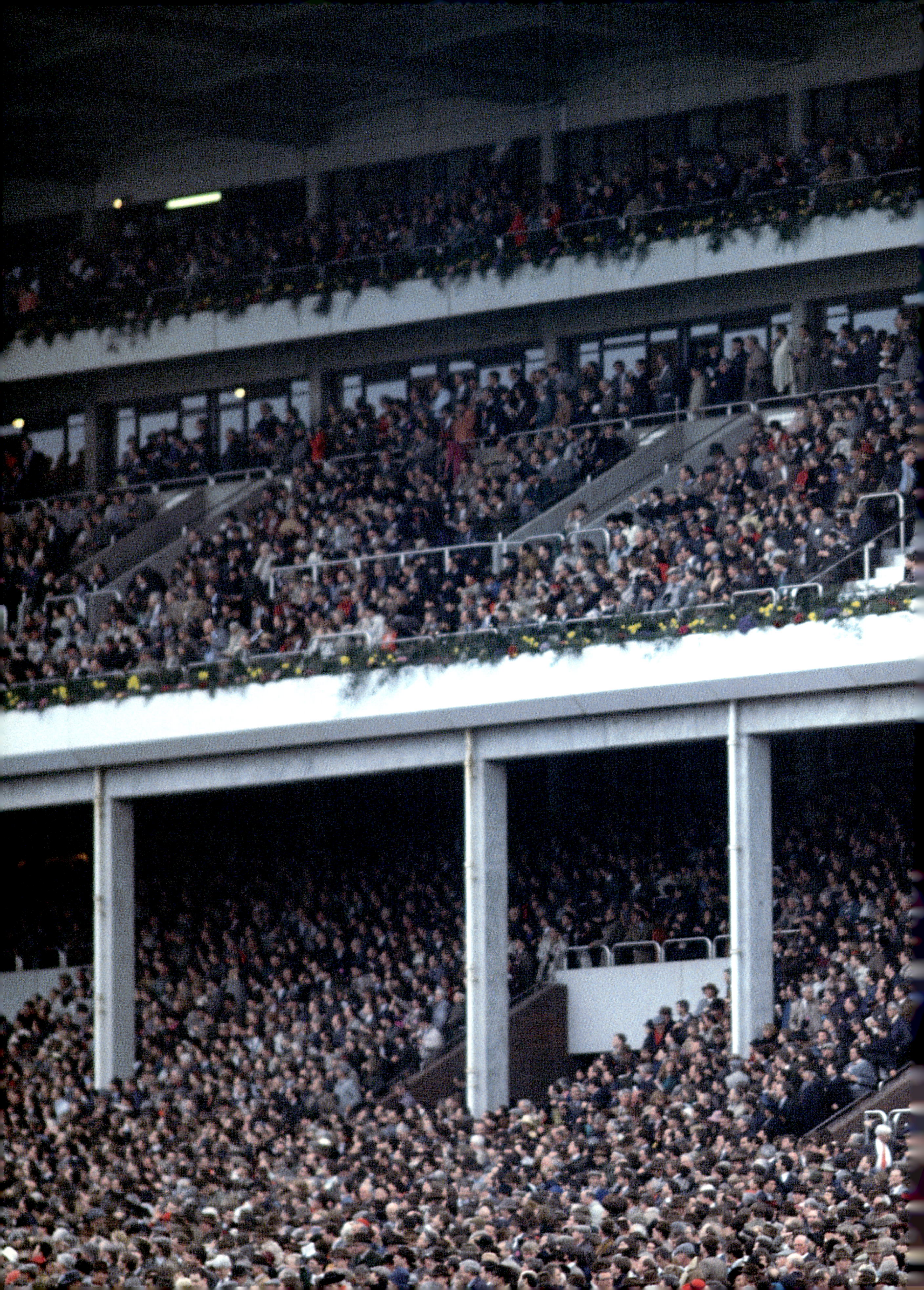

Main photograph: Packed stands.
PHOTOGRAPH: TREVOR JONES.

Inset: Binoculars.
PHOTOGRAPH: TREVOR JONES.

Reflection.
PHOTOGRAPH: ALLSPORT/ PASCAL RONDEAU.

Pat Eddery and Canon Can racing to victory in the K&N Waite Construction Handicap Stakes at Newmarket on 9 August 1996.

Canon supporting the world of sport.

Canon

You and Canon can.

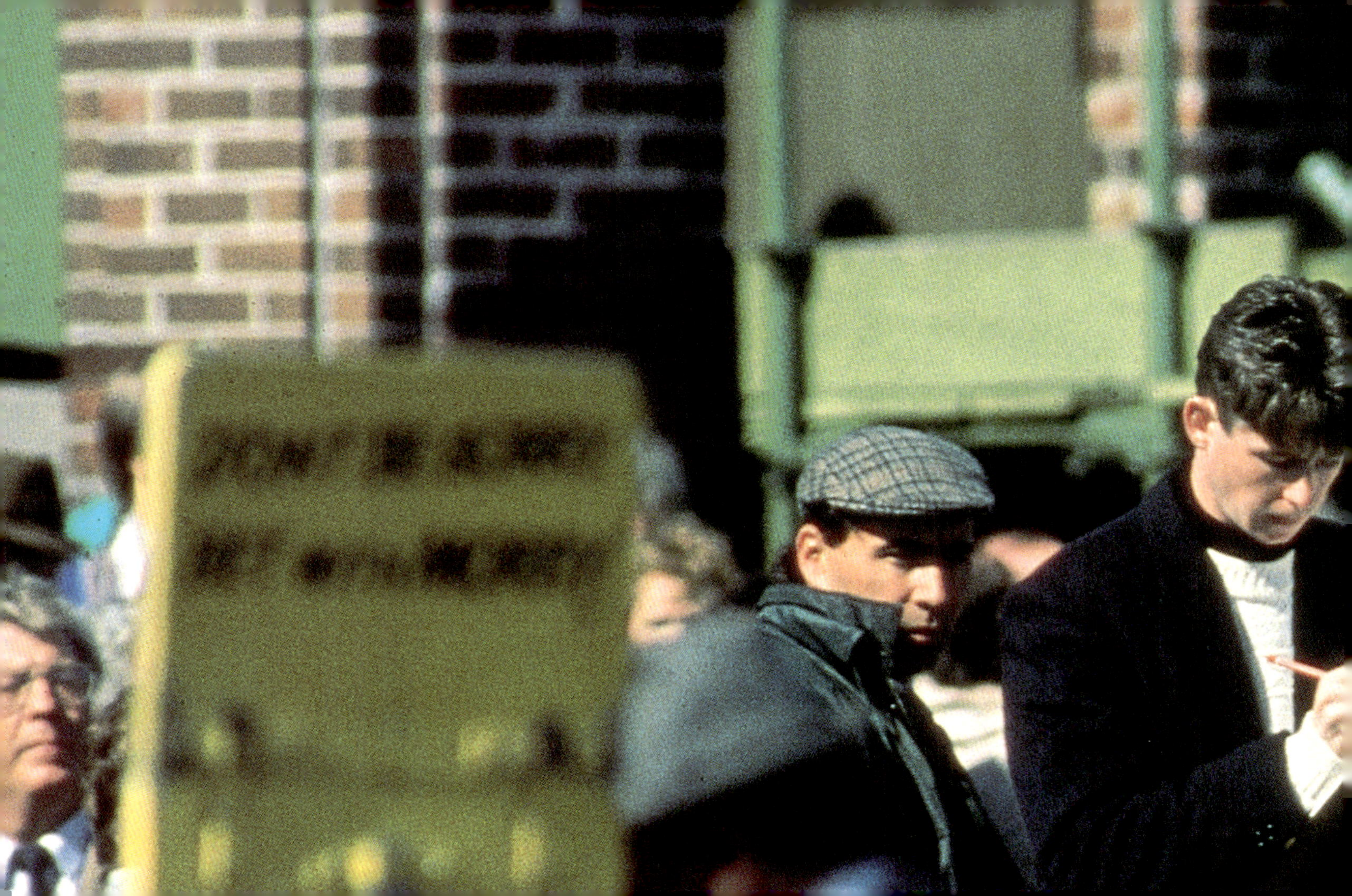

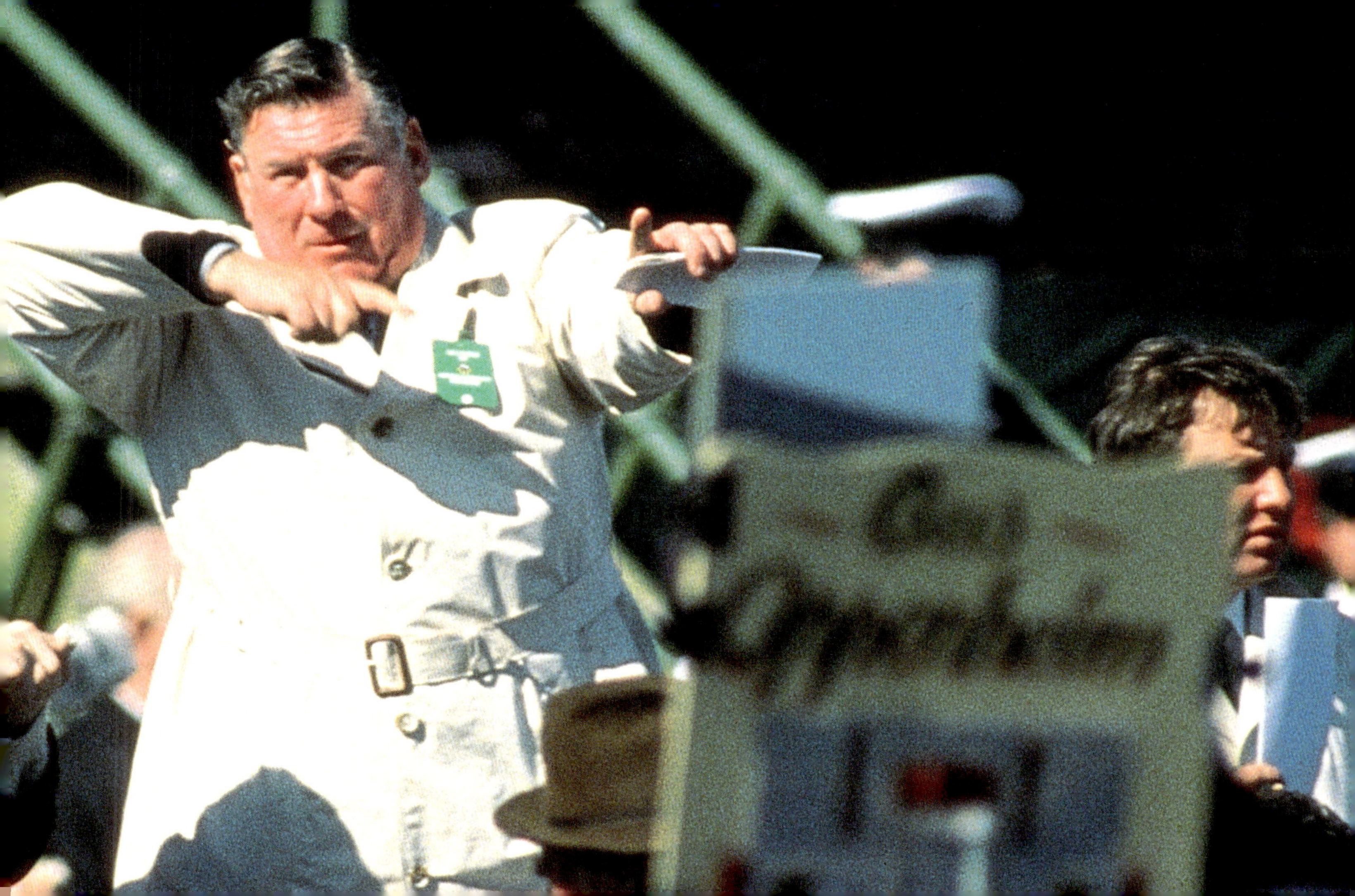

tote
Betting at its best

tote CREDIT CLUB

The best range of bets you can get: SP and Tote odds, Early Prices, Board Prices on every kind of sporting and non sporting event.

5 MORE REASONS FOR JOINING TOTE CREDIT CLUB

- Minimum total stake of only £4 per call.
- Exclusive facilities at all racecourses in the UK.
- Freephone service from within the UK PLUS overseas including France, Ireland, Italy, USA etc.
- Free £10 bet when you join.
- All Tote profits stay in racing

To Join Call Tote Freephone
0800 269188

Tote Credit Club

tote BOOKMAKERS

- Tote and SP Prices on screen.
- Prices on the days Feature Races.
- Betting on all racing, other sporting and non-sporting events.
- Full range of Speciality Bets.
- Quick, and friendly service from experienced staff.

The COMPLETE Betting Service

Off-Course
On-Course

Tote Bookmakers Shops

tote Betting Vouchers

The convenient way to pay for your betting

On-Course Betting – For all Tote Pool Bets

WIN   PLACE   TRIO
DUAL FORECAST
JACKPOT   PLACEPOT
QUADPOT   MULTIBET

Course to Course — Bet and Collect at *any* Window for *all* Meetings

Tote On-Course

Keep up-to-date TOTETEXT C4 pg 567 for Tote Prices
or by INTERNET (http://www.tote.co.uk)

"Eleven to four the field… tens bar two…"

It is the bookies' battle-cry, heard only on British (or Irish) racecourses. Rain or shine, almost every weekday - and, quite a few Sundays too - the bookie stands with his clerk in Tattersalls or the Silver Ring - chalking offered prices on a board and shouting them to a jostle of value-seeking punters.

Close by, leaning on the rails which separate Tatts from the Members', the slightly grander Credit bookies ply their trade - not in ready money but on paper. They include representatives from the leading British bookmakers with whom thousands can be won or lost.

Betting in the noise and bustle of Tatts - looking for and taking a price - you know what you will win. The Tote's dividends, by contrast are decided by the proportion of winning punters. But the Jackpot, Placepot and other pools can pay out a fortune - and to place your bet you need only stand in a queue, not a rugby scrum.

But the gamble is the same - and so is the matchless thrill of cheering home your money. Bookies or Tote… a winner is still a winner.

Previous pages: Lowering the odds.
PHOTOGRAPH: ALLSPORT / DAVID LEAR.

Above: Plenty of choice?
PHOTOGRAPH: ALLSPORT / JON NICHOLSON.

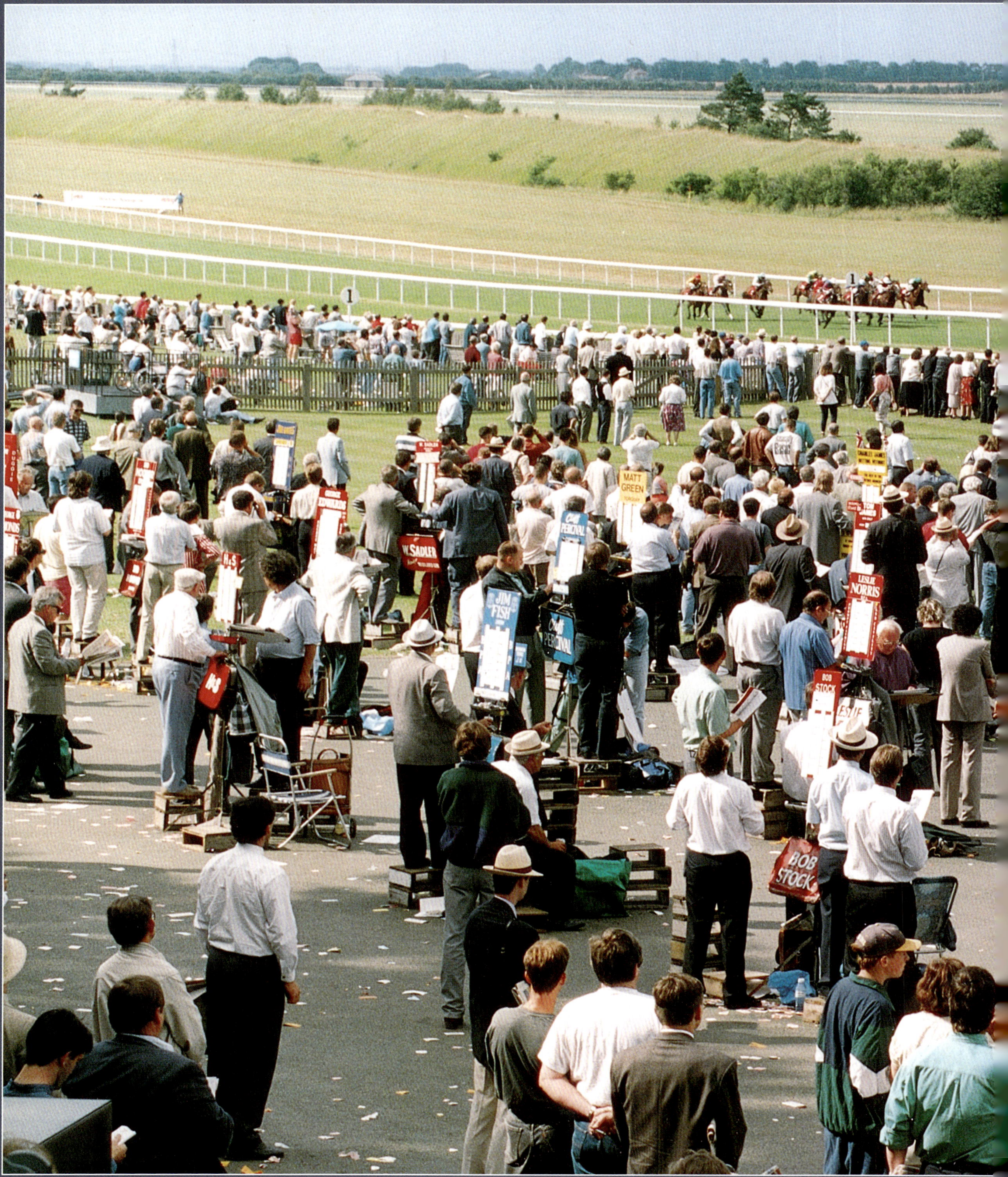

JIM FISH
LESLIE NORRIS
MATT GREEN
BOB STOCK
W. SADLER

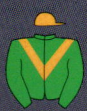

The bookies hold their breath.
PHOTOGRAPH: SPORTSPHOTO.

TOTE BOOKMAKERS
STRATFORD
LINGFIELD
DONCASTER
NEWBURY
JACK
COHEN
W&G
BPA
BPA

Main Photo: Early arrivals.
PHOTOGRAPH: ALLSPORT / SIMON BRUTY.

Inset Above: A lucky punter.
PHOTOGRAPH: DAVID WALTON.

Inset Top Left: Plenty of business for the Tote.
PHOTOGRAPH: TREVOR JONES.

Inset Bottom Left: Six to Four the field.
PHOTOGRAPH: ALLSPORT / SIMON BRUTY.

Rail bookmakers coin it in.
PHOTOGRAPH: TREVOR JONES.

KIM C. BAILEY
Leading National Hunt Trainer

Pictured with Champion Hurdle winner, Alderbrook

The Old Manor
Upper Lambourn
Hungerford
Berkshire RG17 8RG

Tel: 01488 71483
Fax: 01488 72978

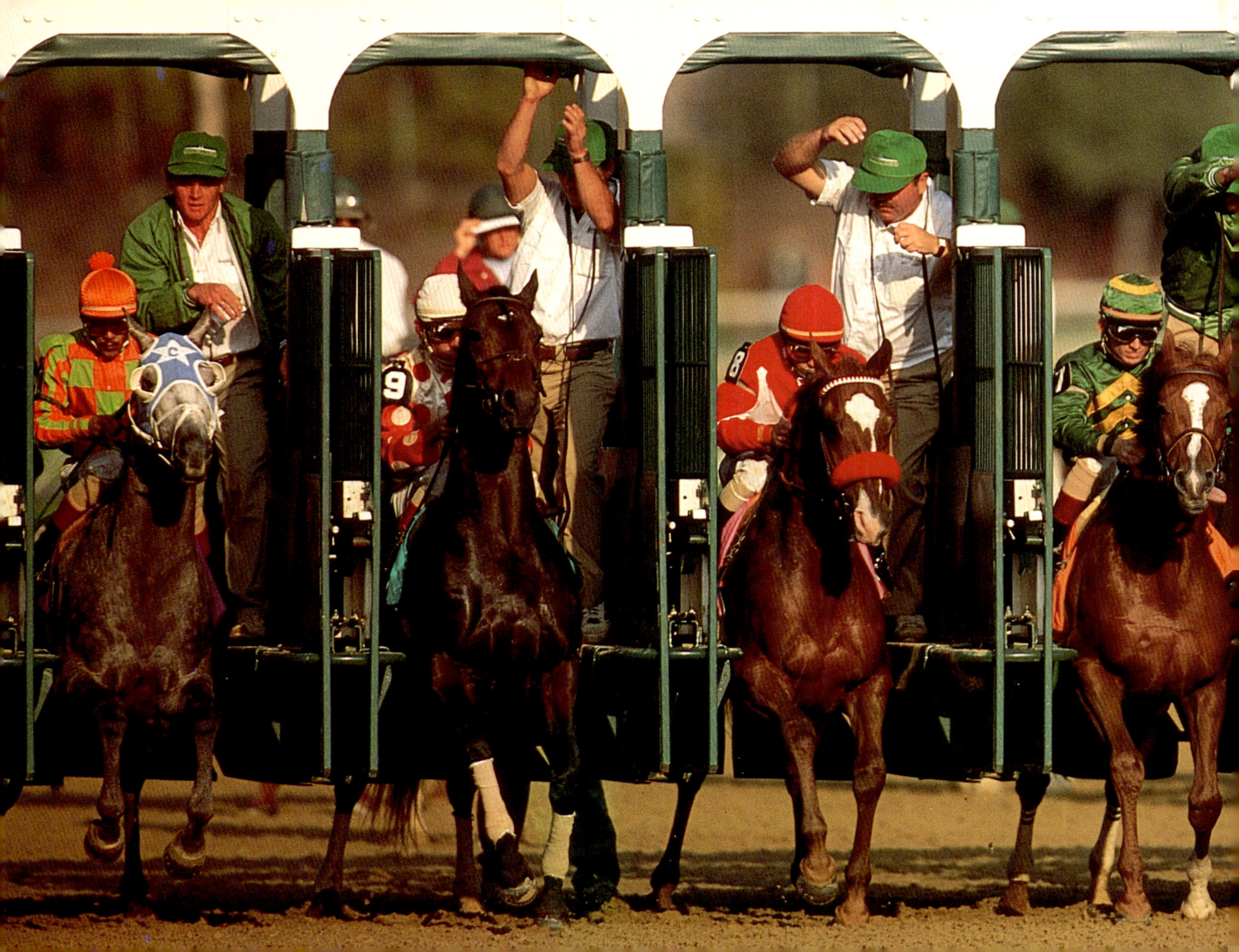

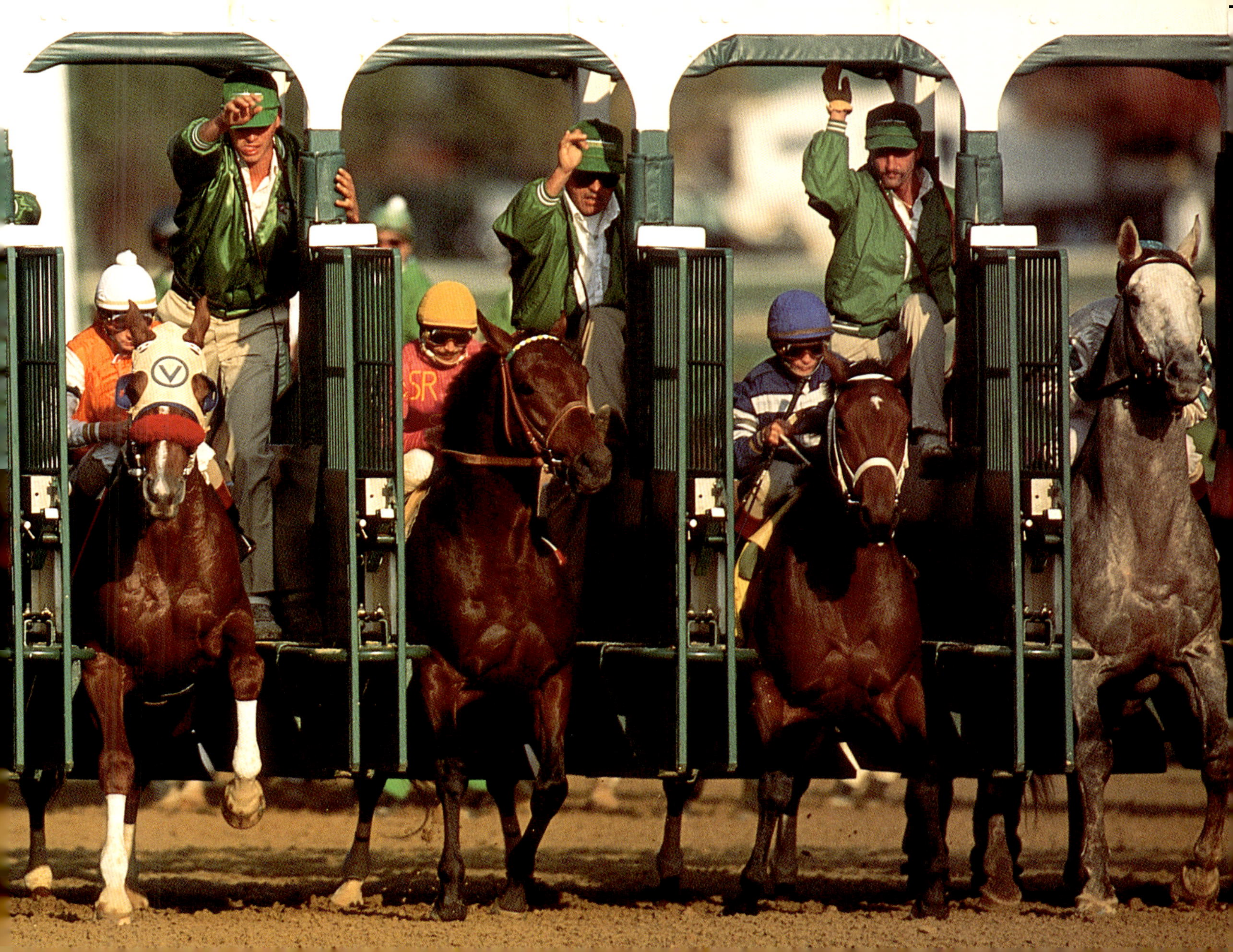
SR

WHITBREAD

WINNING COLOURS

Pizza Hut

Thresher

Brewers Fayre

Marriott
Hotels · Resorts · Suites

T.G.I. Friday's

Beefeater
Restaurant & Pub

40 years sponsoring the Gold Cup

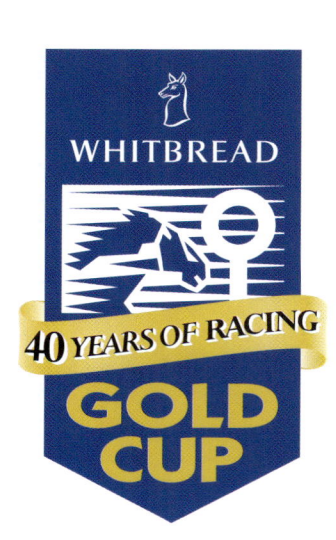

WHITBREAD
40 YEARS OF RACING
GOLD CUP

250 years of business innovation

"Nerves travel down the reins" they say

- but even horses with nerveless riders know when a race is coming up. They feel it in the horsebox, at the racecourse stables, the Parade Ring - and when the jockey is legged-up wearing colours (recognisable even if it is true that horses are colour blind) they know for certain.

The jockey knew long ago - and may have been riding the race in his mind, or dreams, for weeks. How fast will they go? Will his horse pull? Will it jump? Will it like the ground? Will it be good enough to win?

Owner, trainer and punters are anxiously asking themselves those questions in the stands. But the answers hang on split second tactical choices made by the jockey - and his rivals.

Should I make the running and if not, how long can I wait? Is there room between those horses - when should I make my move?

Dettori and Dunwoody may make riding winners look easy. Don't you believe it…

Previous pages: The start.
PHOTOGRAPH: TREVOR JONES.

Above: Helping hands encourage a nervous horse into the stalls.
PHOTOGRAPH: MISS L DAVIDGE.

Inset top: A certain hesitancy is apparent before the start!
PHOTOGRAPH: MISS L. DAVIDGE.

Inset Middle: The weighing room at Longchamps.
PHOTOGRAPH: TREVOR JONES.

Inset Bottom: Eager for the fray.
PHOTOGRAPH: GRAHAM ELY.

Main Photograph: Sighting the horse. Tokyo
PHOTOGRAPH: ALLSPORT / ANTON WANT.

127

Right: Upset at the start of the Sun Alliance Chase.
PHOTOGRAPH: TREVOR JONES.

Below: Derby Day.
PHOTOGRAPH: ALLSPORT / BEN RADFORD

Far Right: The Starter.
PHOTOGRAPH: TREVOR JONES.

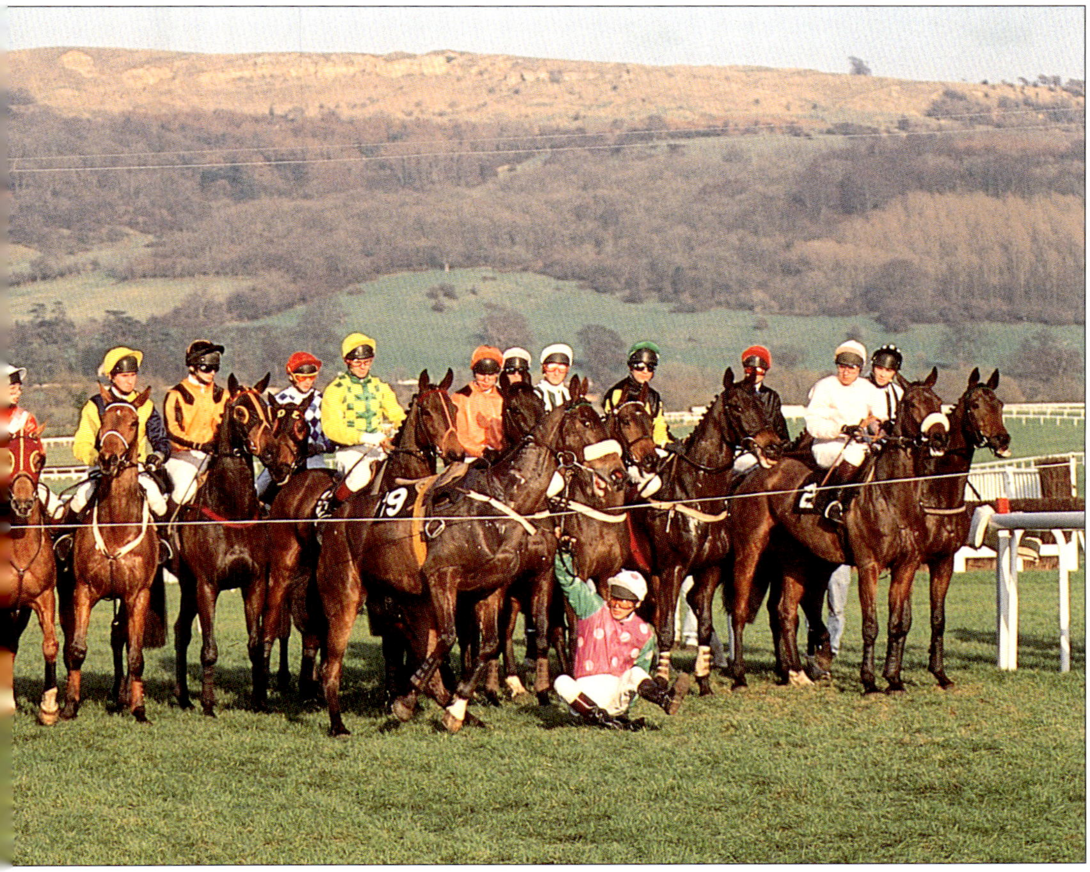

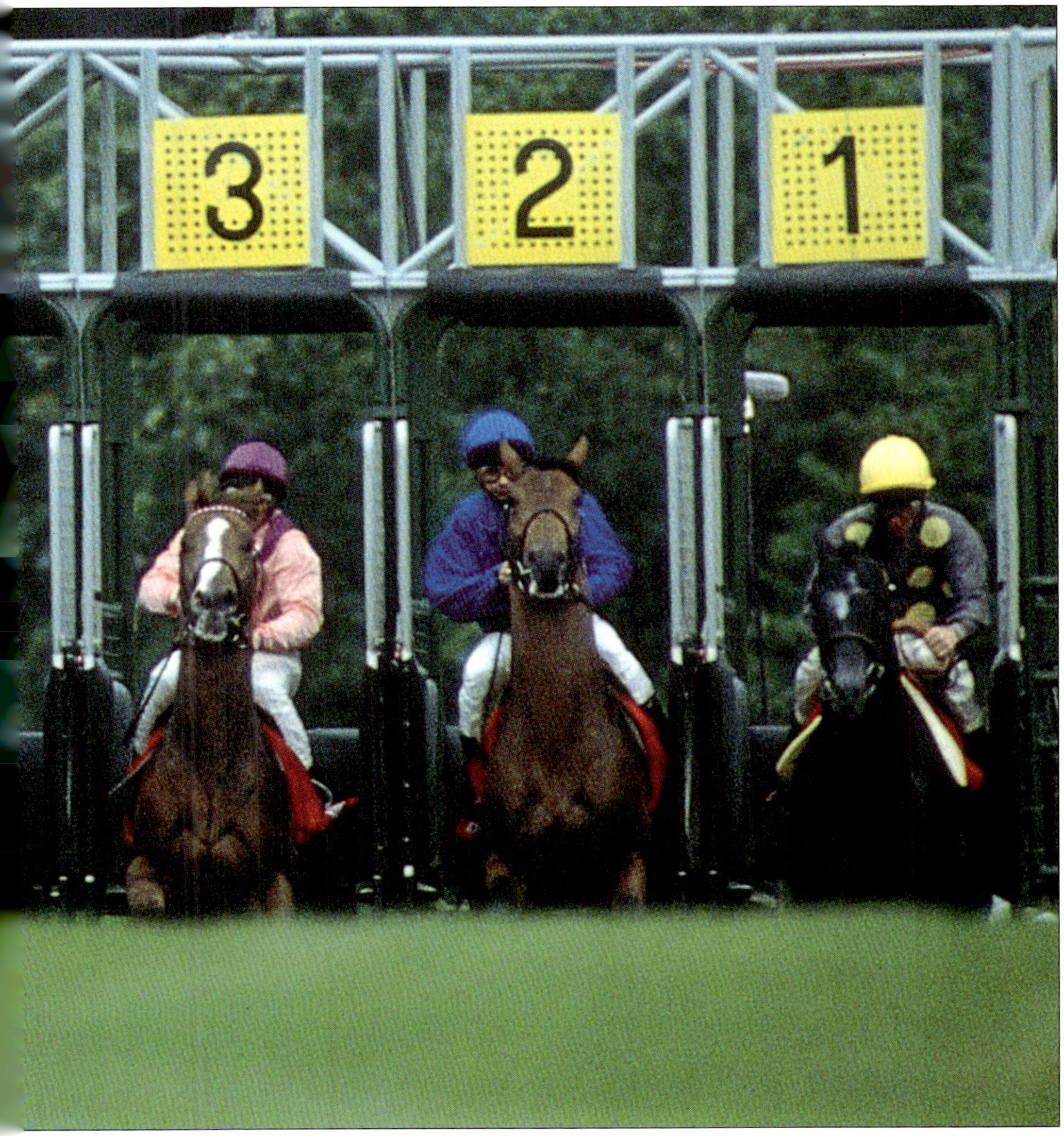
3
2
1

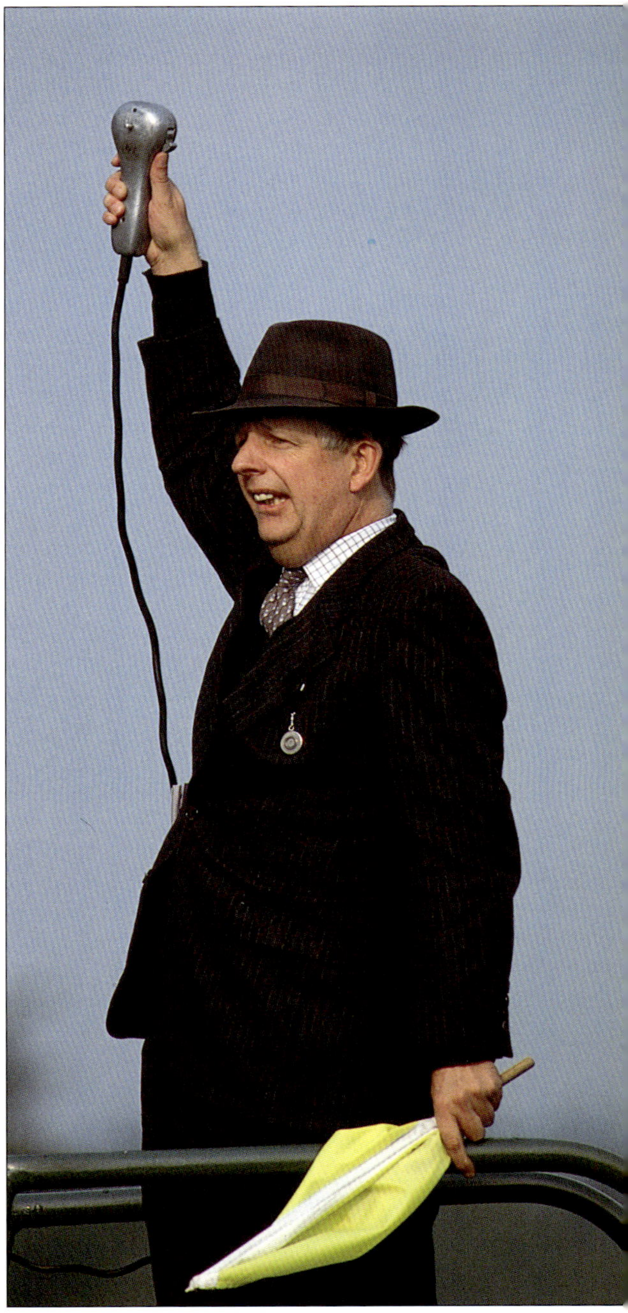

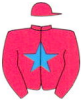

Main photograph: Power.
PHOTOGRAPH: ALLSPORT / PASCAL RONDEAU.

Inset above: 'Out of the blocks'.
PHOTOGRAPH: TREVOR JONES.

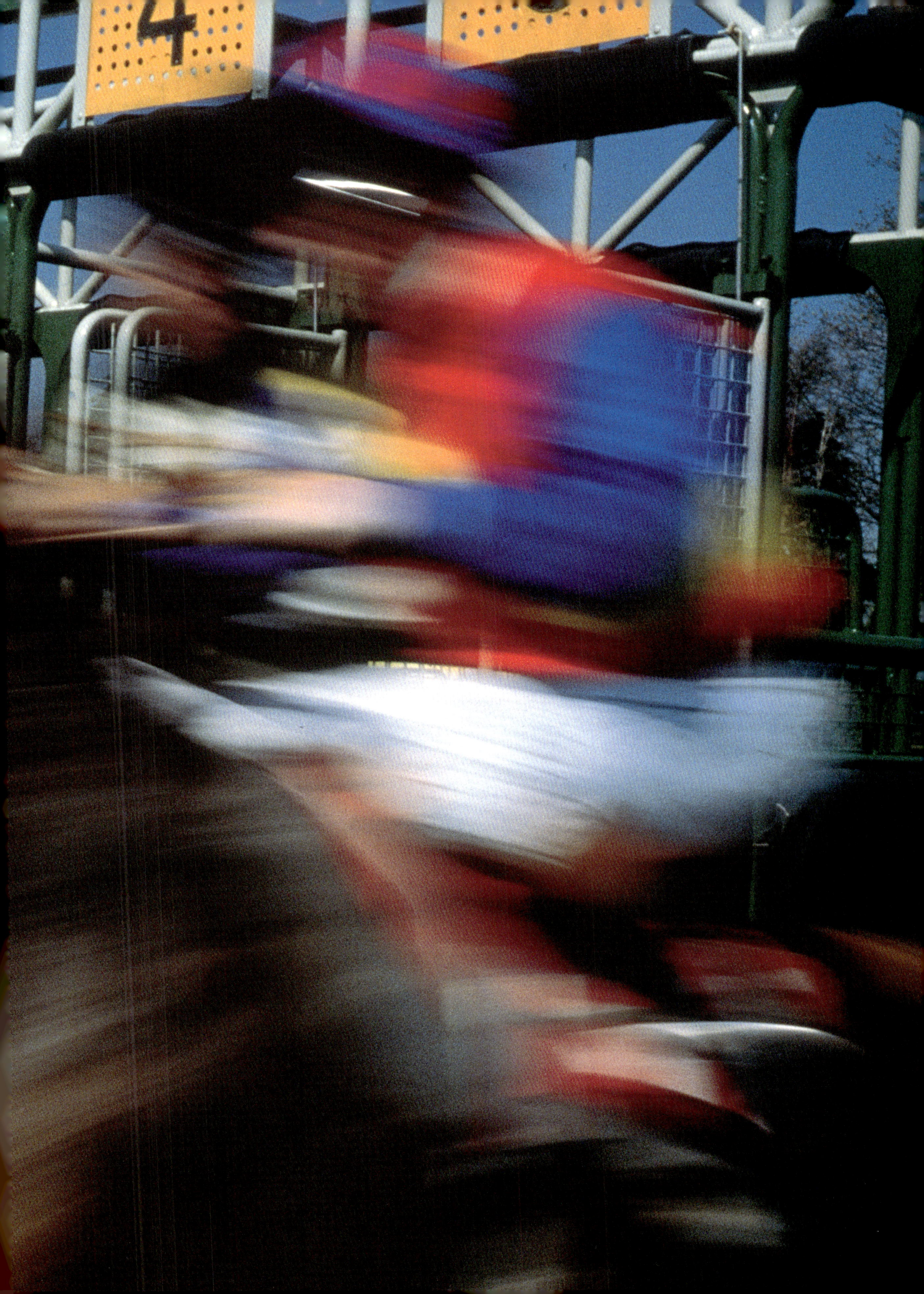
4

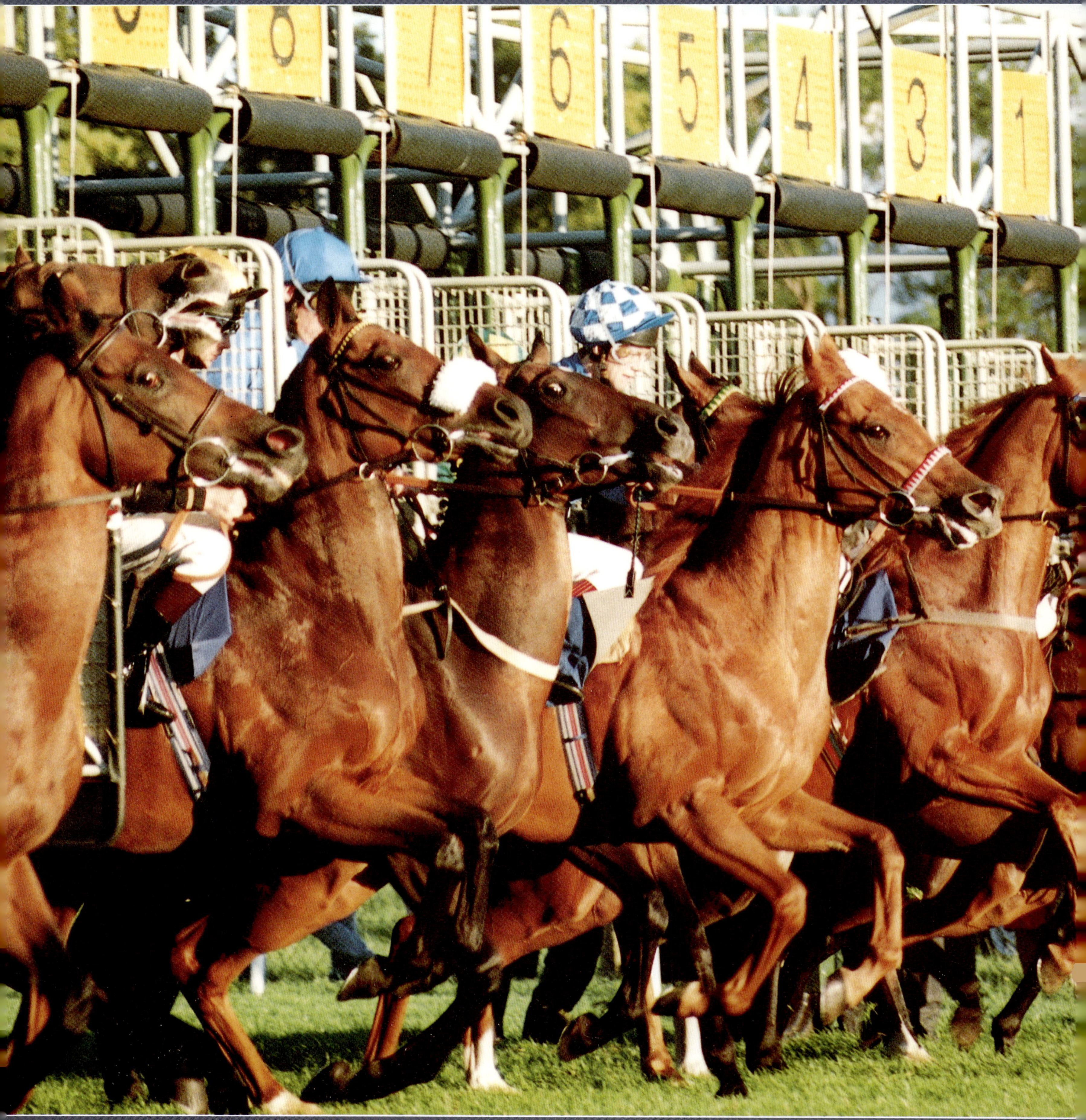

8
7
6
5
4
3
1

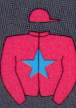

Above: Lanfranco Dettori.
PHOTOGRAPH: TONY EDENDEN / SPORTSPHOTO.

Left: 'They're off!'
PHOTOGRAPH: SUE ORPWOOD.
(1ST PRIZE IN THE MOODS OF HORSE RACING PHOTOGRAPHIC COMPETITION).

Next pages: Churchill Downs, USA.
PHOTOGRAPH: TREVOR JONES.

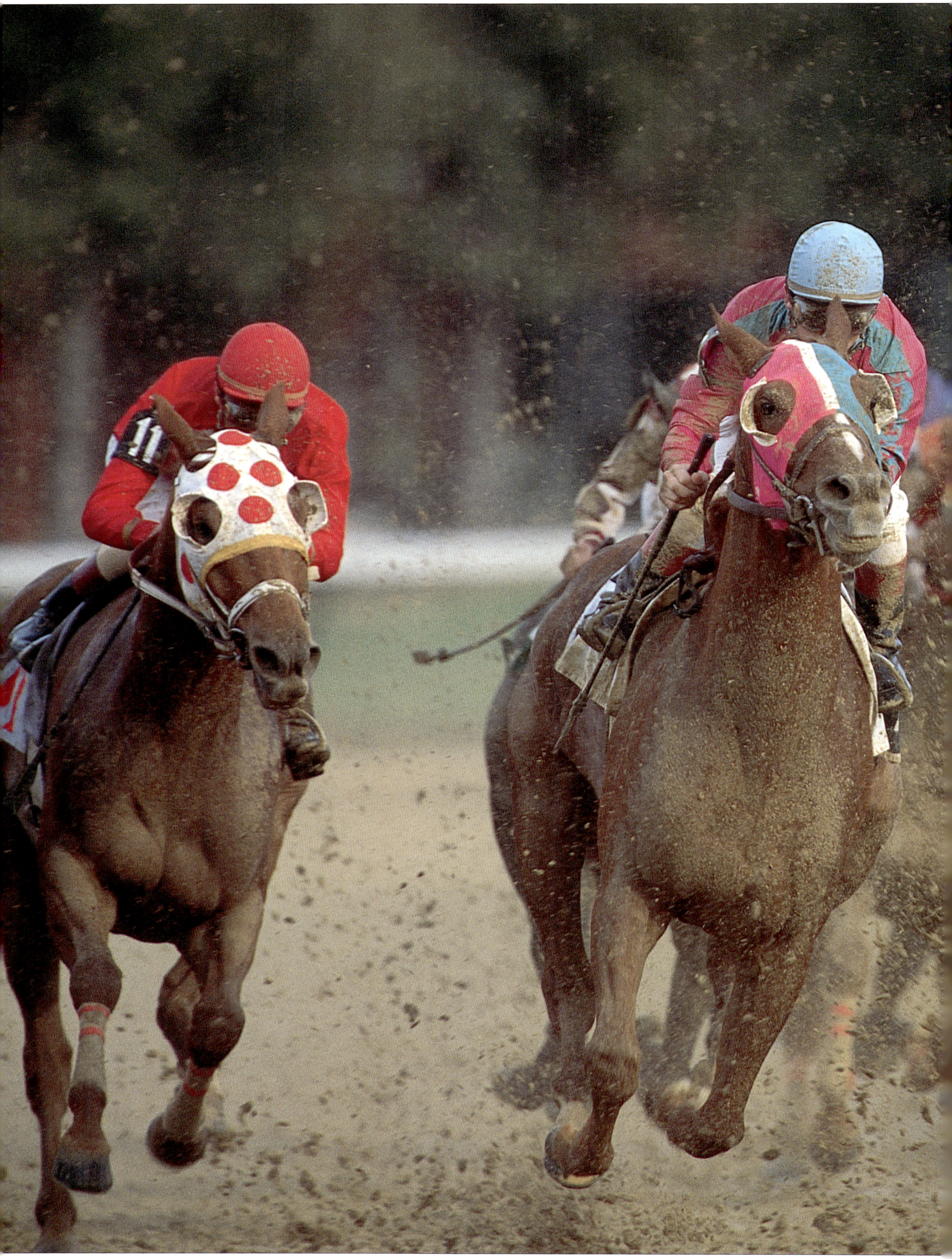
11

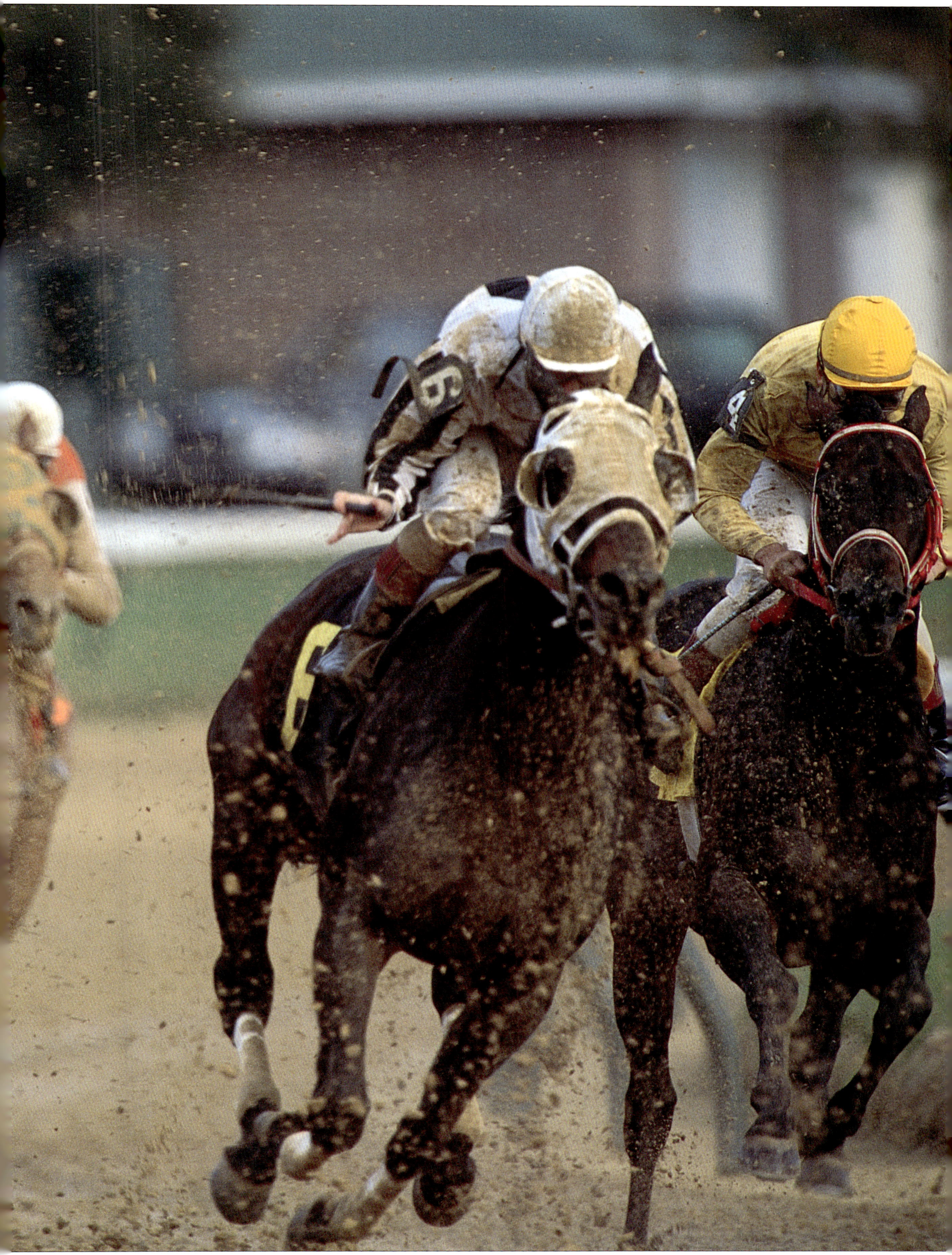
6
4

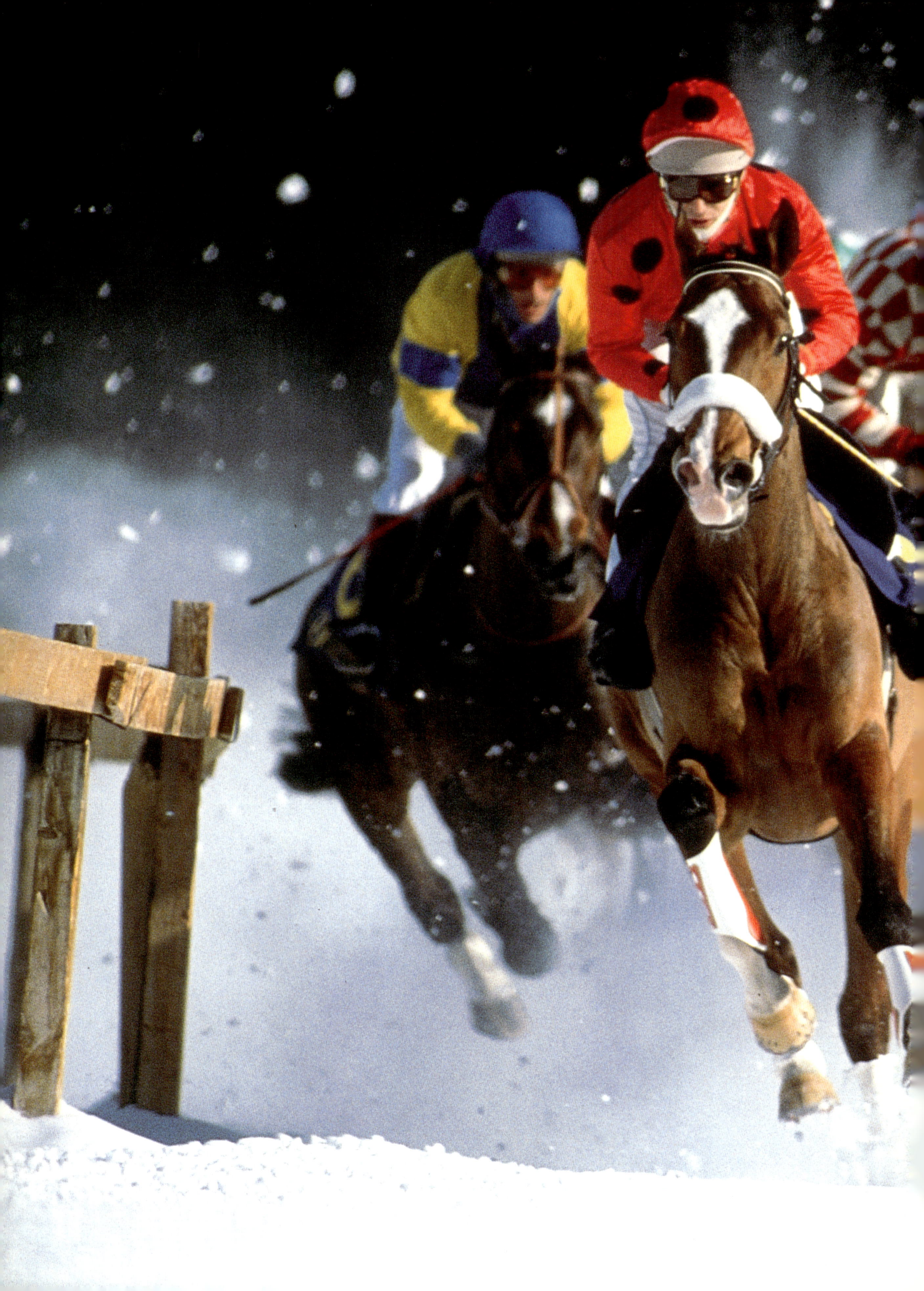

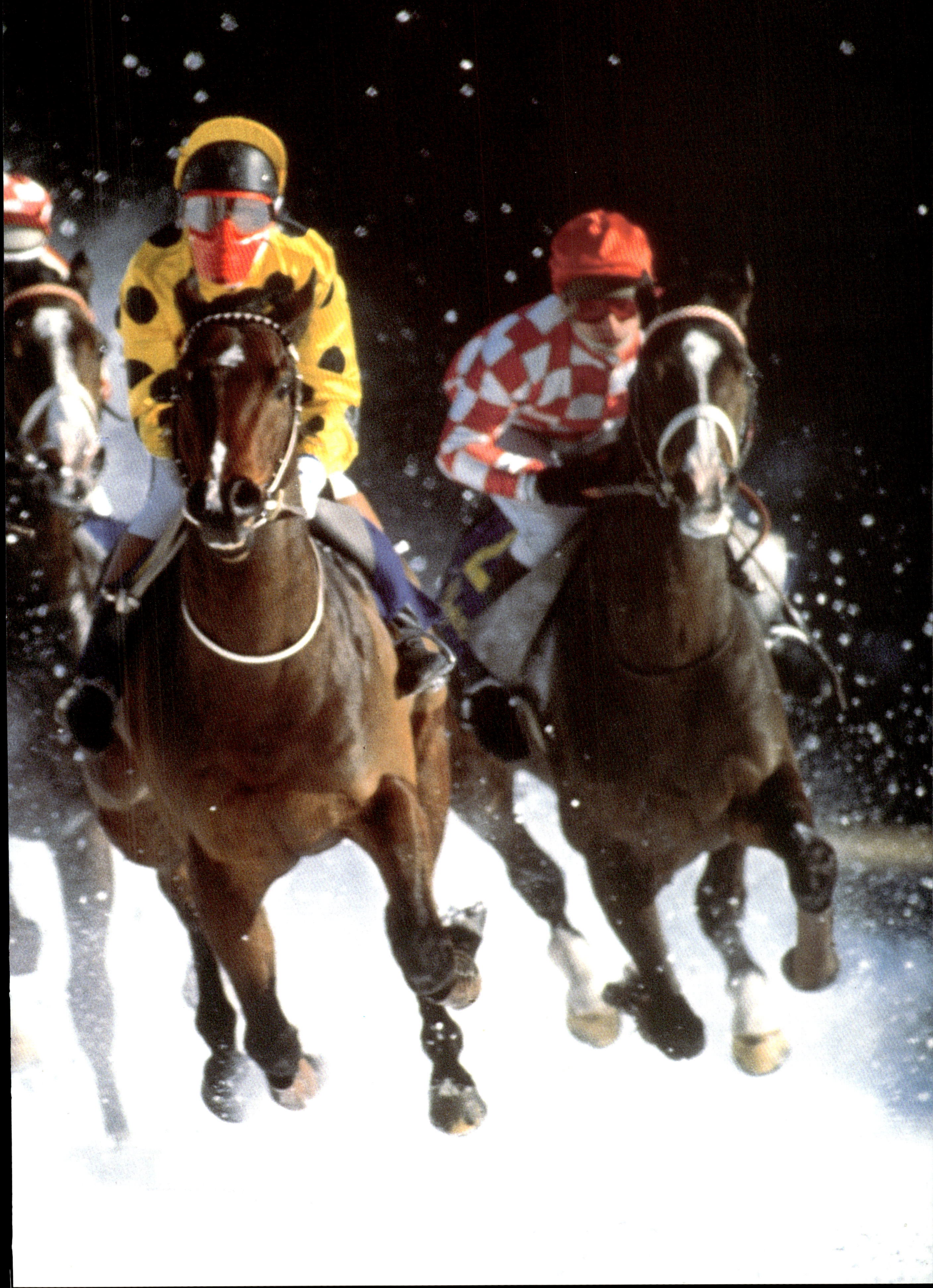

Previous pages: Racing in the snow at St Moritz.
PHOTOGRAPH: ALLSPORT.

Main Photograph: Aintree.
PHOTOGRAPH: ALLSPORT / MIKE HEWITT.

Inset: Two ways to take a fence!
PHOTOGRAPH: TREVOR JONES.

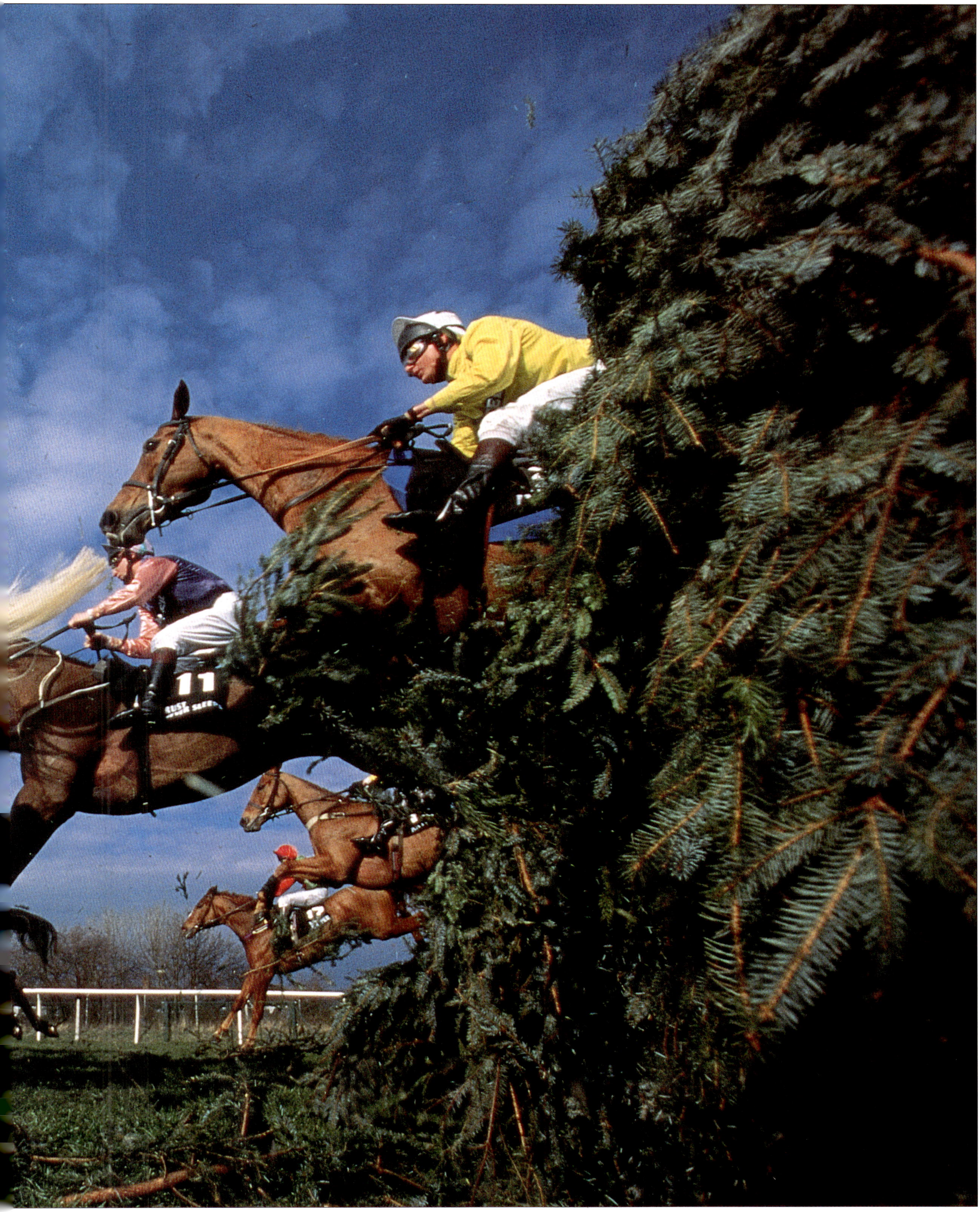

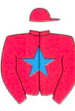

Cheltenham.
PHOTOGRAPH: TREVOR JONES.

The stunning setting for the racetrack at Chantilly.
PHOTOGRAPH: TREVOR JONES.

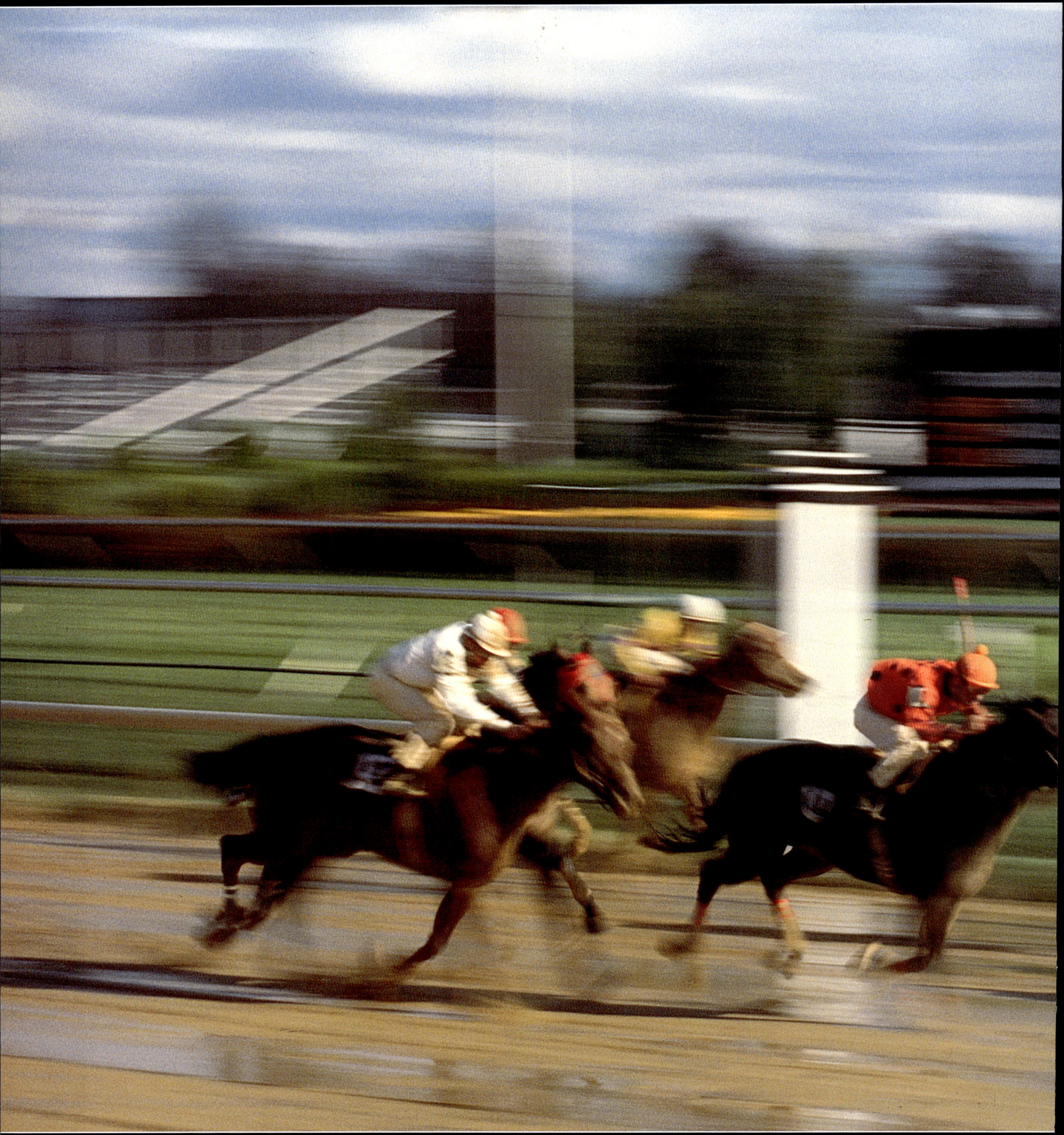

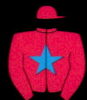

Dirt-track racing in the USA.
PHOTOGRAPH: TREVOR JONES.

Above: Lingfield All-weather track.
PHOTOGRAPH: TREVOR JONES.

Main photograph: Close encounter.
PHOTOGRAPH: ALLSPORT.

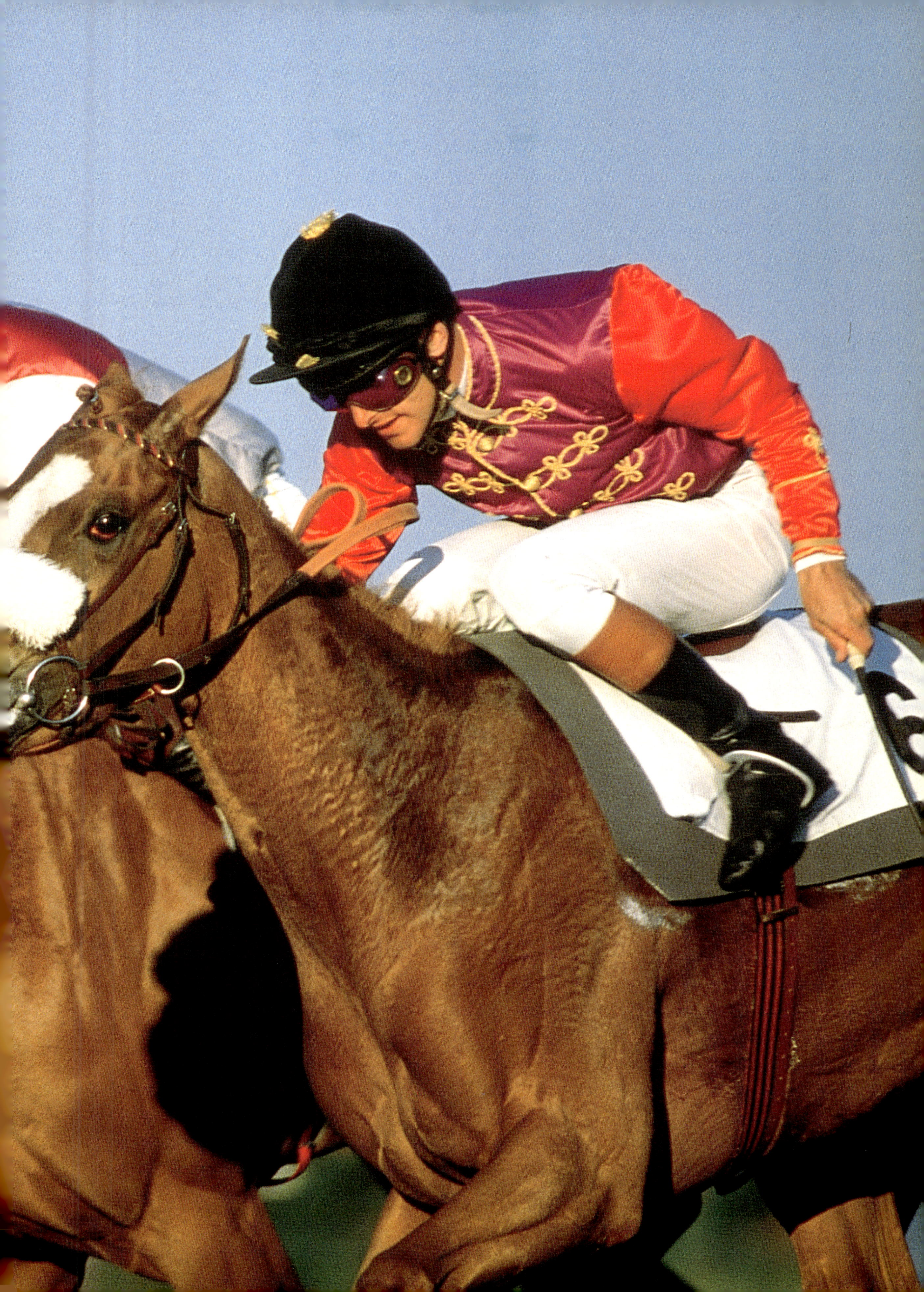

Below: A close-run race.
PHOTOGRAPH: TREVOR JONES.

Inset Right: Touching down.
PHOTOGRAPH: ALLSPORT.

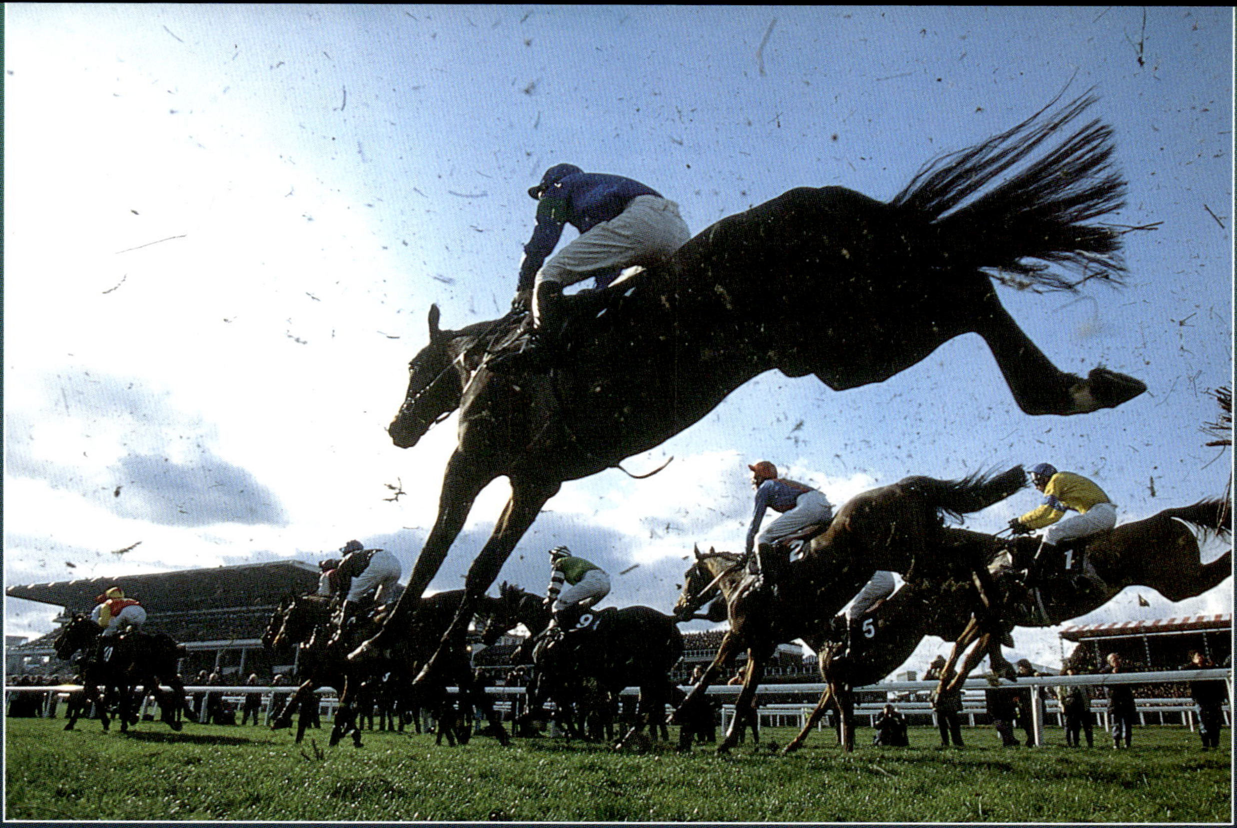
DANKA
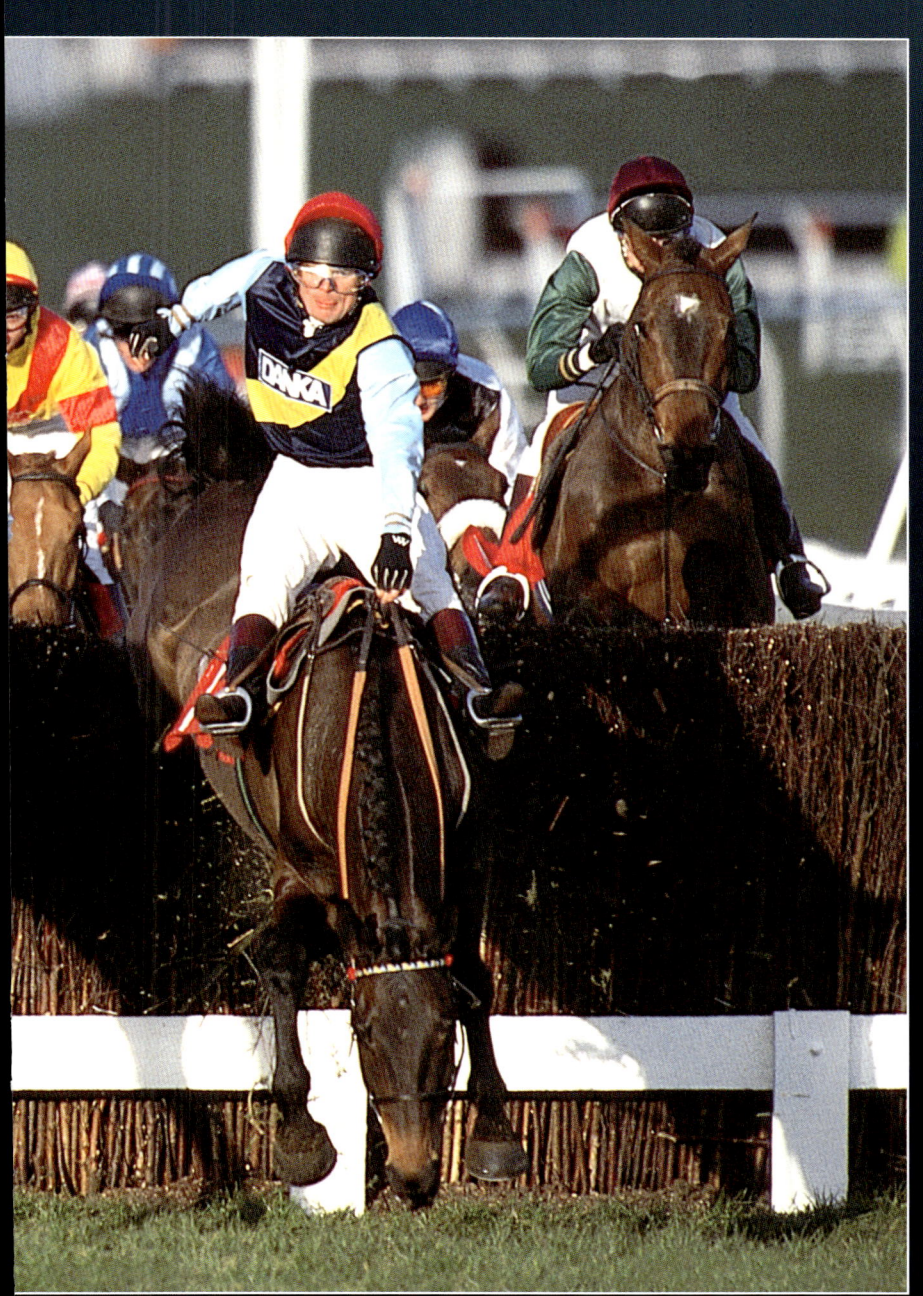

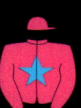

Above: Charlie Swan comes a cropper.
PHOTOGRAPH: ALLSPORT / DAVE ROGERS.

Right: Even a Champion jockey doesn't always get it right. A dramatic fall but Tony McCoy and Brigadier Supreme survived.
PHOTOGRAPHS: W EVERITT.

Next pages: Silhouette. Fontwell Park.
PHOTOGRAPH: ALLSPORT / PHIL COLE

HILL
INSTANT FREEPHONE
0800 44

HILL
INSTANT

HILL
INSTANT

HILL

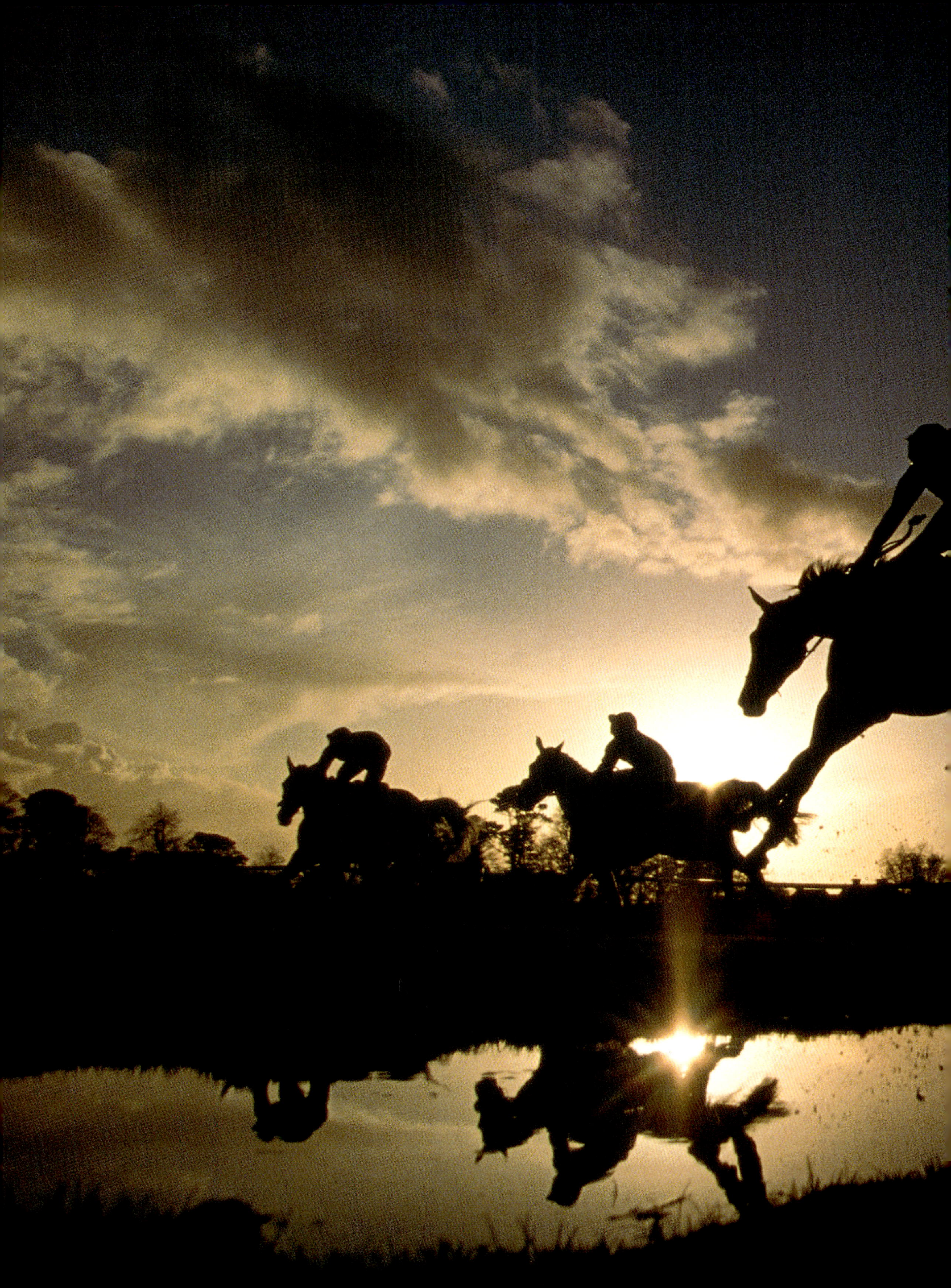

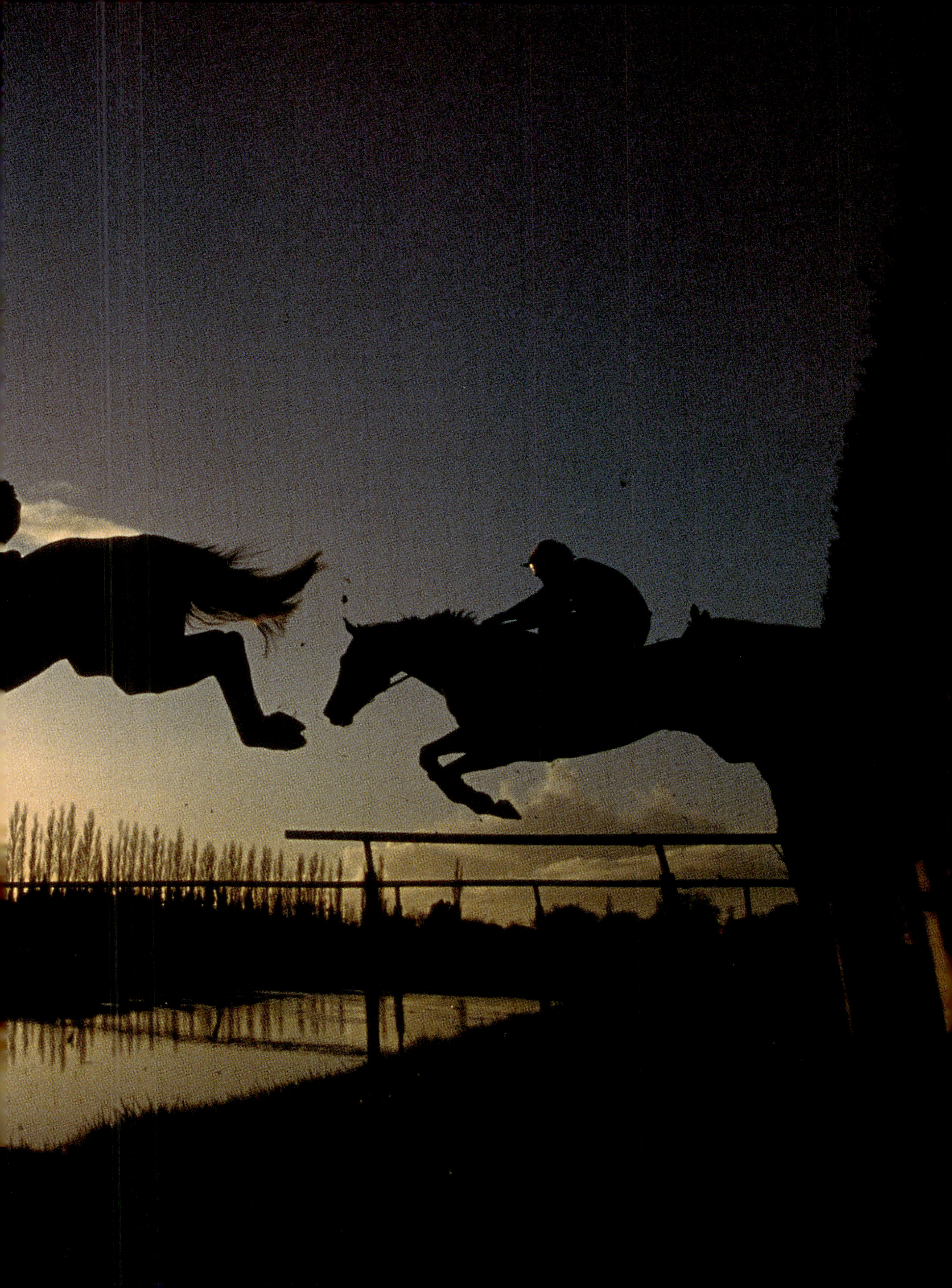

The pack gives chase in Tokyo.
PHOTOGRAPH: ALLSPORT / ANTON WANT.

153

Chester.
PHOTOGRAPH: TREVOR JONES.

Racing on the sand at Laytown in Ireland.
PHOTOGRAPH: TREVOR JONES.

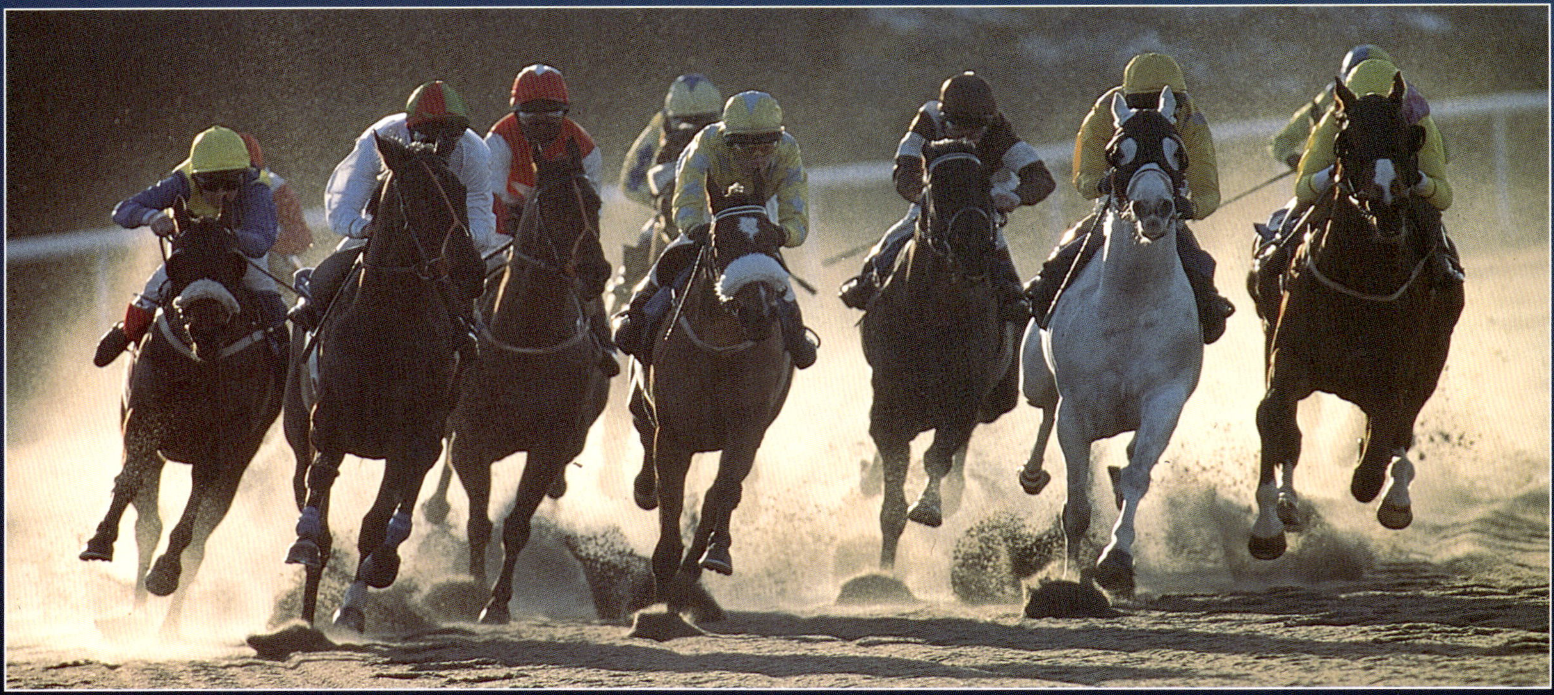

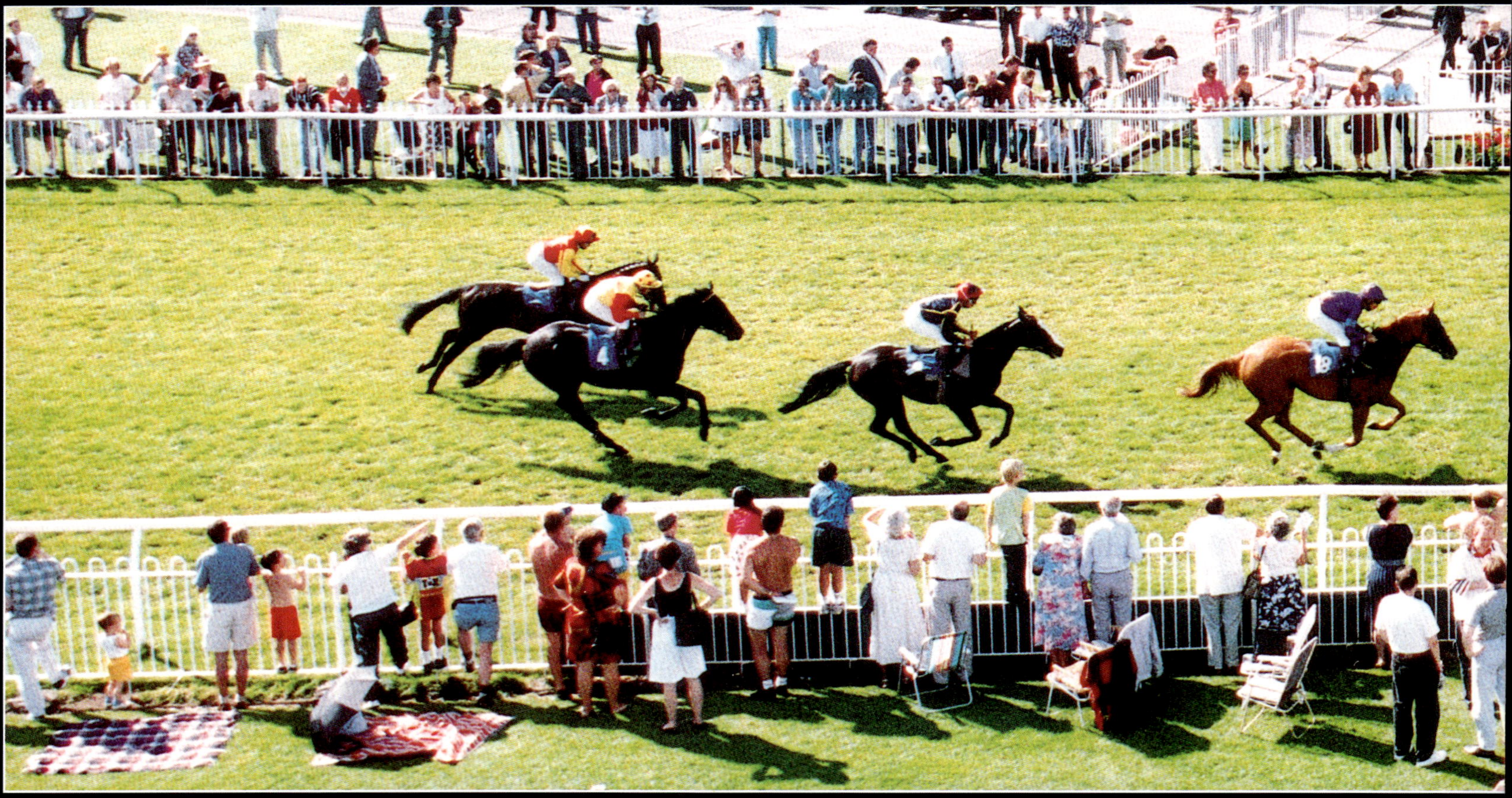

Left: The field raises the dust at Lingfield.
PHOTOGRAPH: ALLSPORT / ANTON WANT.

Below: First past the post at Ripon.
PHOTOGRAPH: SPORTSPHOTO / TONY EDENDEN.

Above: Winning is hot work.
PHOTOGRAPH: SUE ORPWOOD.

Right: The end of the race at Santa Anita.
PHOTOGRAPH: TREVOR JONES.

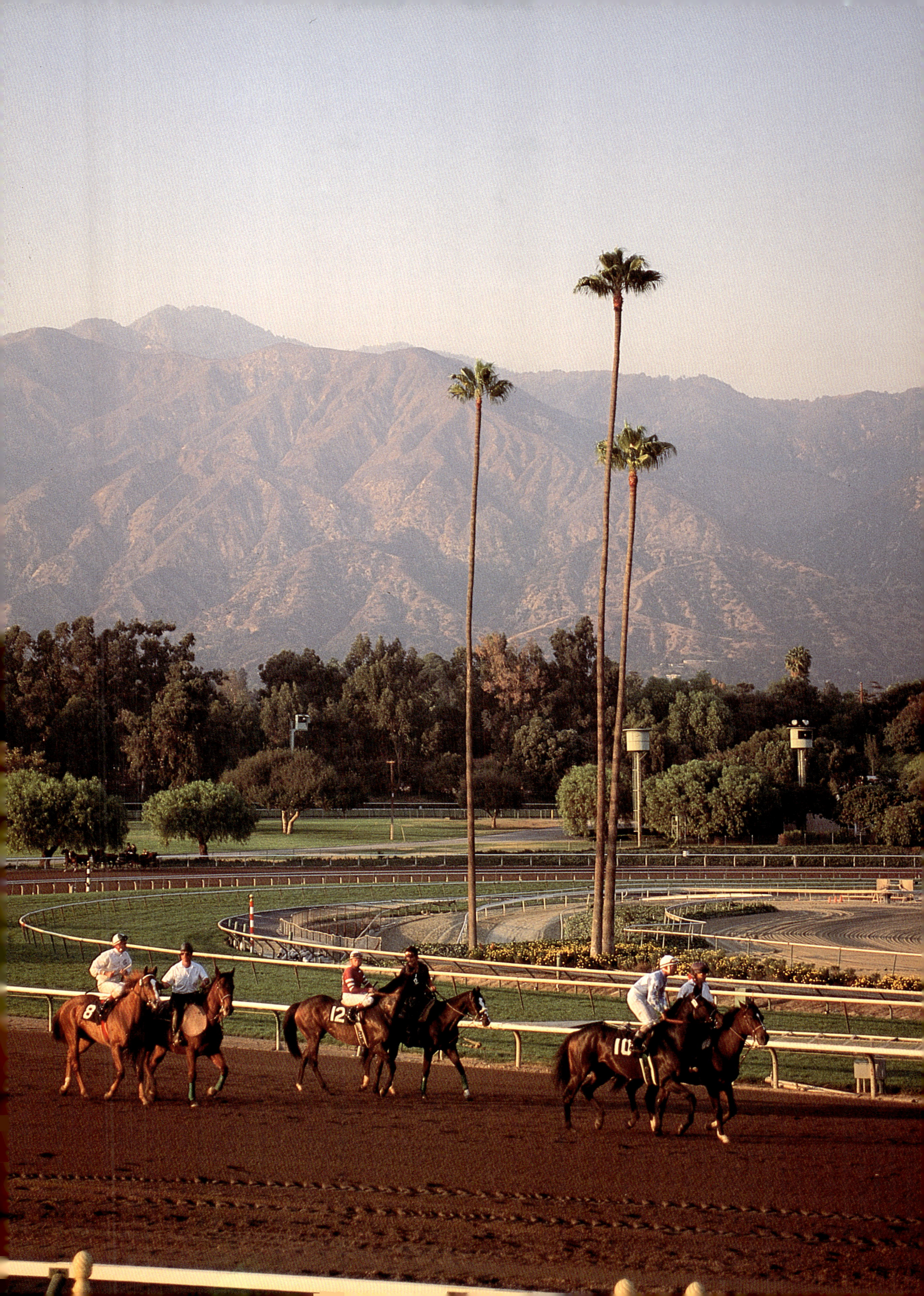

The Winners

PHOTOGRAPH: TREVOR JONES.

...from the land of *thoroughbreds*

A *stable* of award winning desktop printers

♦ Laser ♦ Inkjet ♦ Matrix

For printing in mono, full colour, Bay, Black, Chestnut or Grey

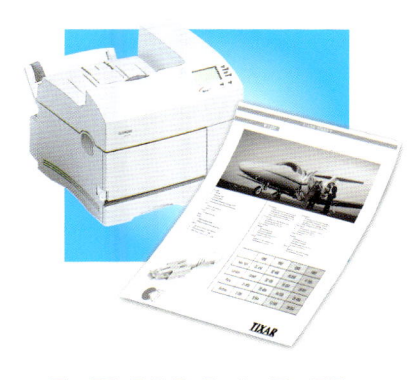

We have the *breeding*
We have the *technology*

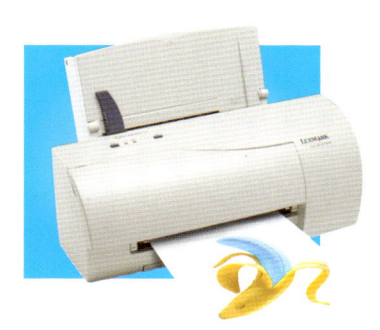

LEXMARK - ALWAYS IN THE WINNER'S CIRCLE

Lexmark International Ltd.,
Westhorpe House, Little Marlow Road, Marlow, Buckinghamshire SL7 3RQ
Telephone: 01628 481500   Fax: 01628 481886   http://www.lexmark.co.uk

PRINT LEXMARK

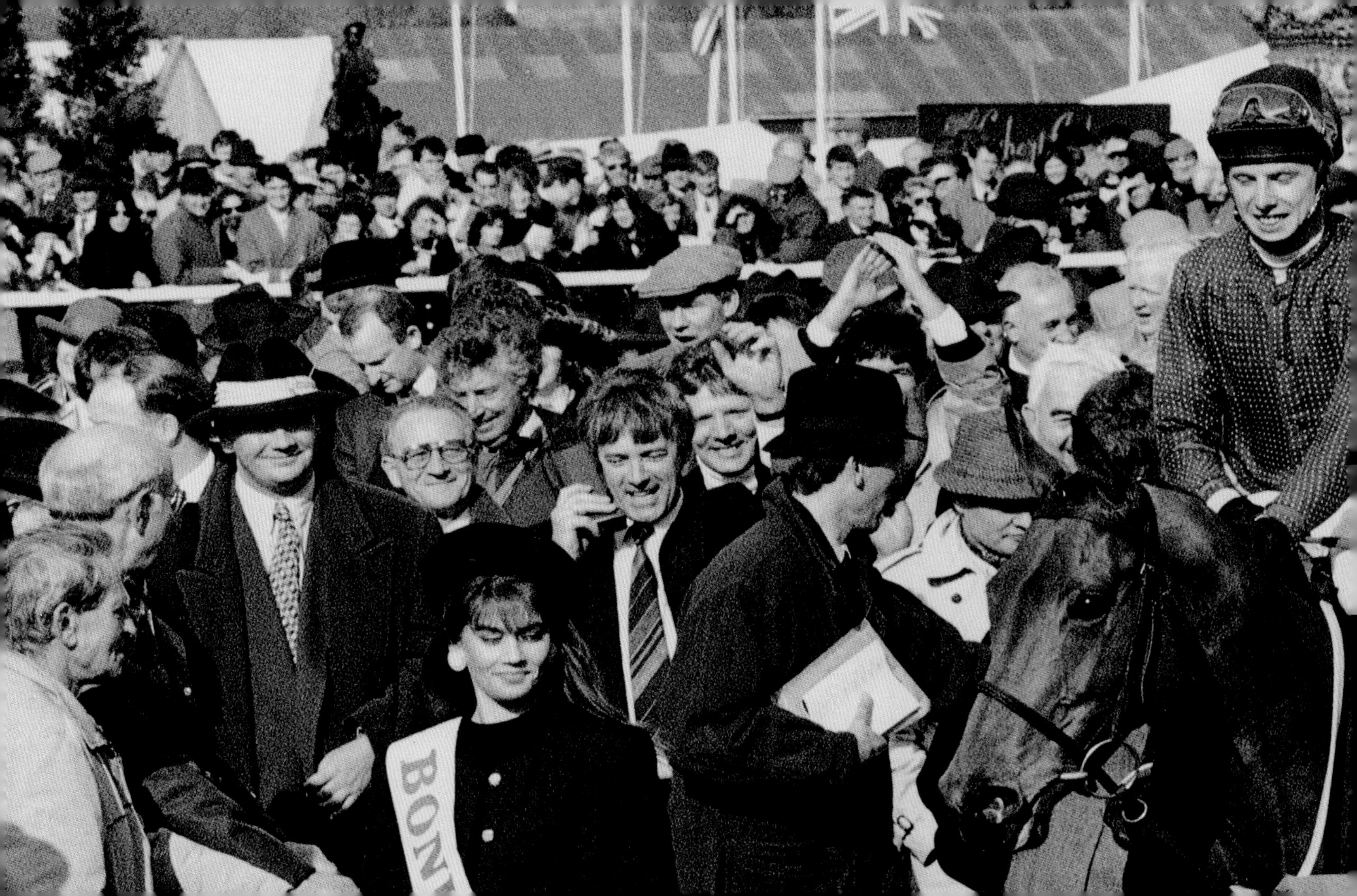
BON

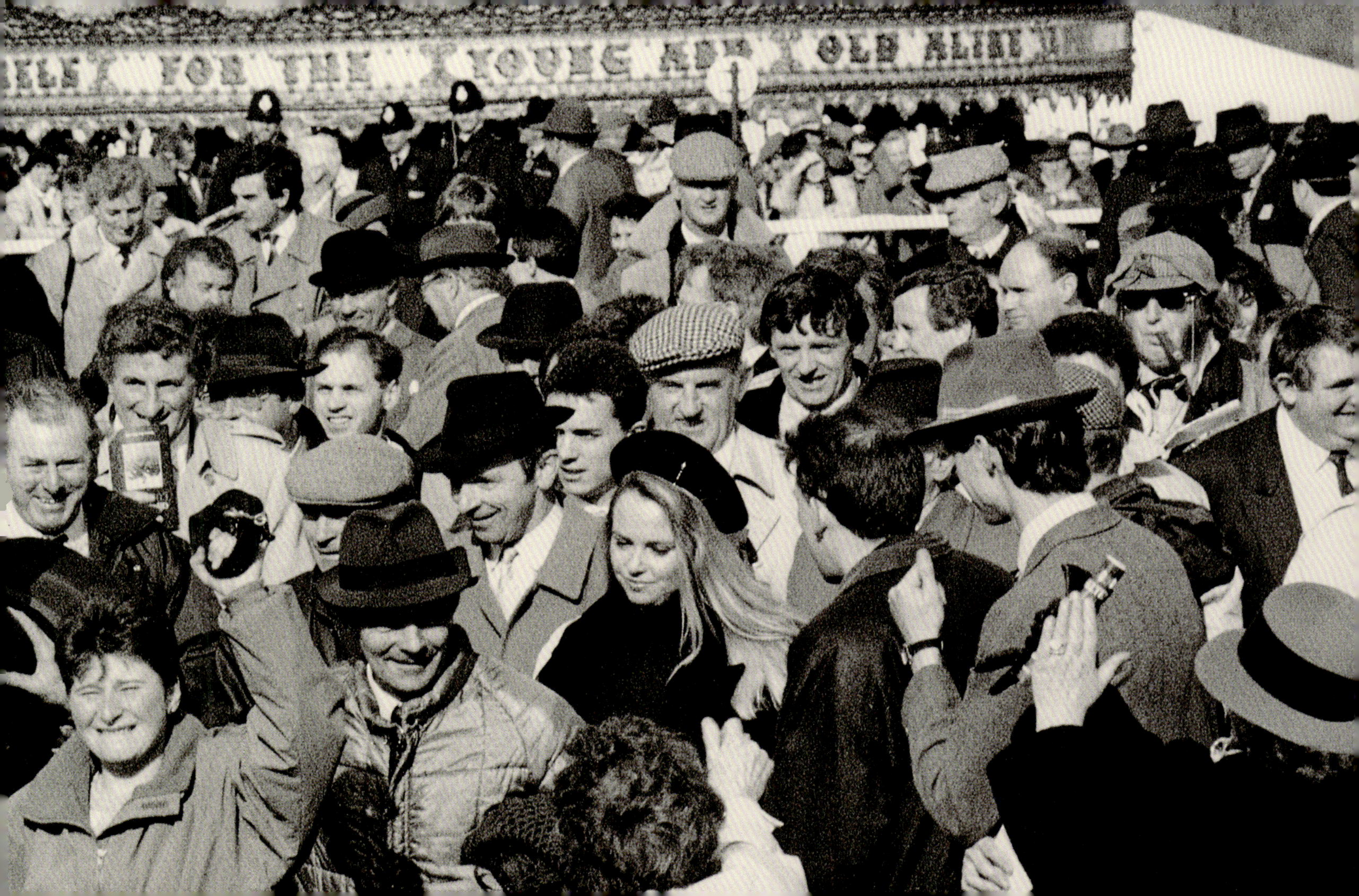
FOR THE YOUNG
OLD ALIKE

THE BEST BET
BY APPOINTMENT
TO HER MAJESTY QUEEN ELIZABETH II
PURVEYORS OF CHAMPAGNE LANSON
PÈRE ET FILS · REIMS
CHAMPAGNE
DEPUIS 1760
Lanson
à REIMS FRANCE
BLACK LABEL
BRUT
ÉLABORÉ PAR LANSON PÈRE ET FILS · REIMS · FRANCE
CHAMPAGNE
Lanson

Previous pages: Success.
PHOTOGRAPH: JOHN CHASE.

Above: Frankie Dettori wins the King George VI and Queen Elizabeth Diamond Stakes.
PHOTOGRAPH: W EVERITT.
(WINNER OF CHAPTER PRIZE)

It is winning that counts in racing.

True, you get a prize for coming second - and perhaps a bit of 'gallant loser' credit. But the record books are filled with lists of winners. So are the racing papers. It is the winner everyone remembers.

Just watch the faces in the unsaddling enclosures. You will see the difference. Champagne smiles in one - resignation or resentment in the others. Natural good losers are rare and some jockeys (and trainers) are better with their alibis than others.

Of course there is always another day and, if they come back safe without disgrace, that's enough to satisfy some owners.

But what about the trainer? He has evening stables and tomorrow morning to look forward to - knowing, too well, the catalogue of possible disasters.

'Those legs look all right now and he walked back sound enough. But the ground *was* bloody firm whatever they said. Put the bandages on quickly and Please God let him be OK tomorrow…'

Main Photograph: A winning lady.
PHOTOGRAPH: TREVOR JONES.

Inset right: Peter Scudamore prepares to celebrate.
PHOTOGRAPH: TINA WHITE.

Inset Middle Right: Urubande and Charlie Swan celebrate a Cheltenham victory.
PHOTOGRAPH: IAN YATES.

Inset Far Right: Granville Again wins Champion Hurdle.
PHOTOGRAPH: TREVOR JONES.

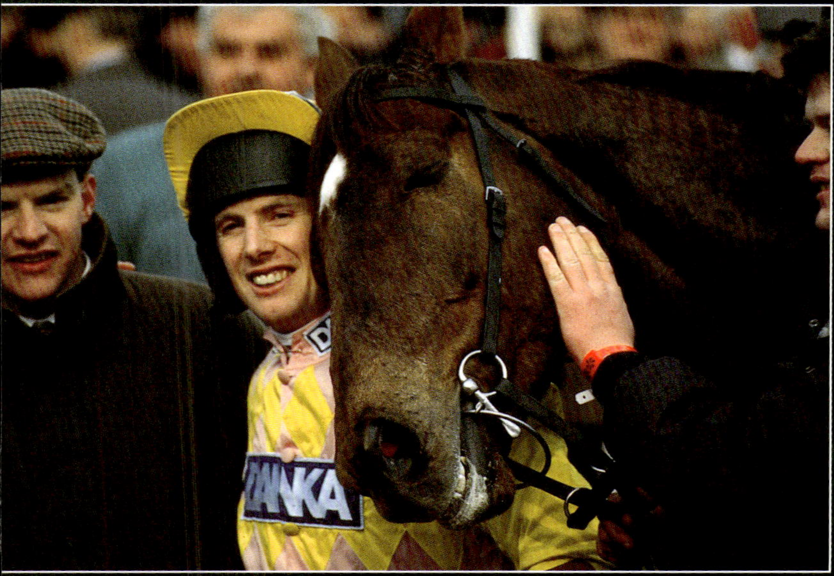

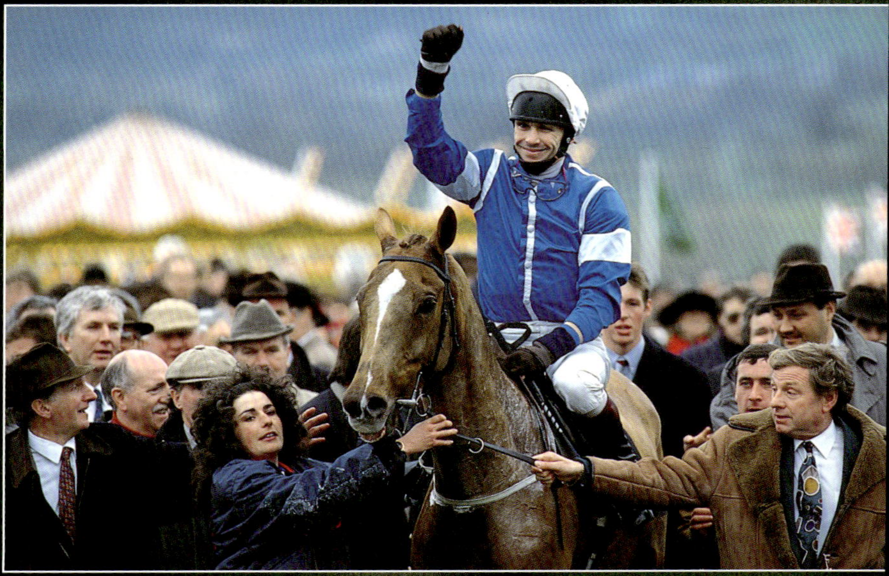

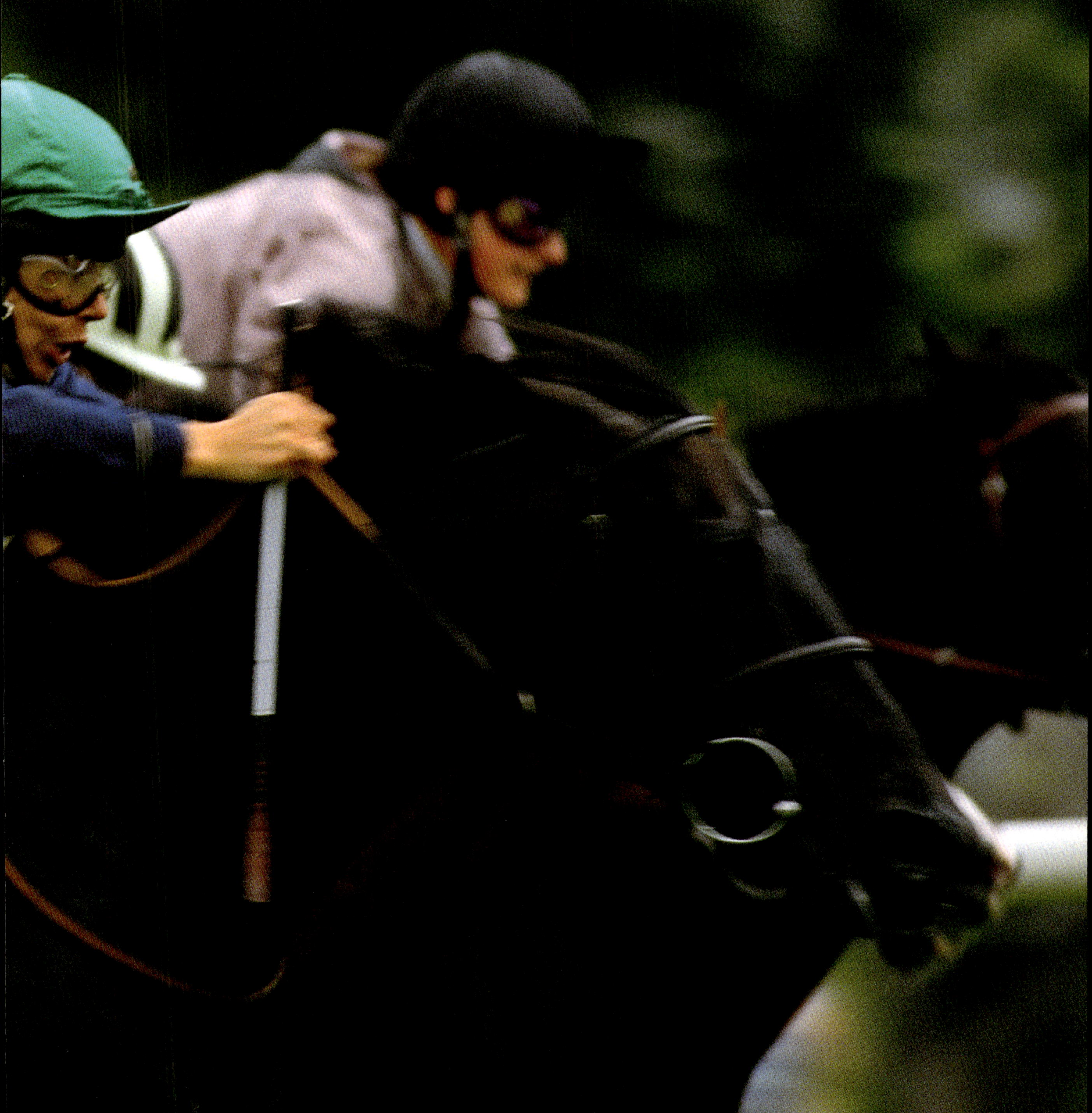

Above: Mr Frisk wins the Grand National for Kim Bailey and together they enjoy a champagne breakfast.
PHOTOGRAPH: MATTHEW WEBB.

Left: Dermot Whelan receives the Trainer's Trophy at Kempton Park.
PHOTOGRAPH: DAVID HASTINGS.

Above Right: Celebration time.
PHOTOGRAPH: JOHN CHASE.

Right: Tattersalls Tiffany Trophy.
PHOTOGRAPH: TREVOR JONES.

Far Right: Willie Haggas wins the Derby.
PHOTOGRAPH: J L SALMOND.

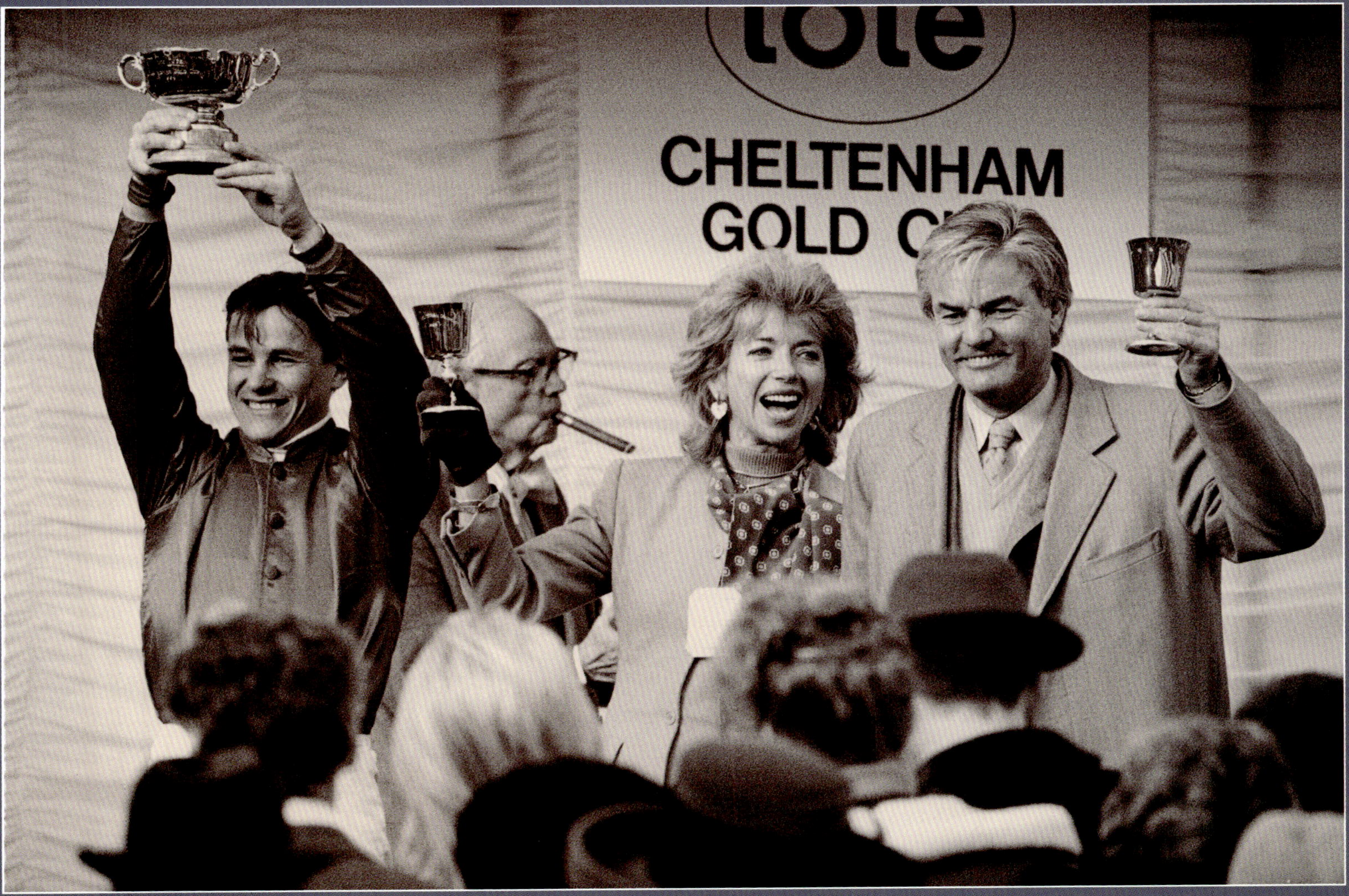
tote
CHELTENHAM
GOLD C

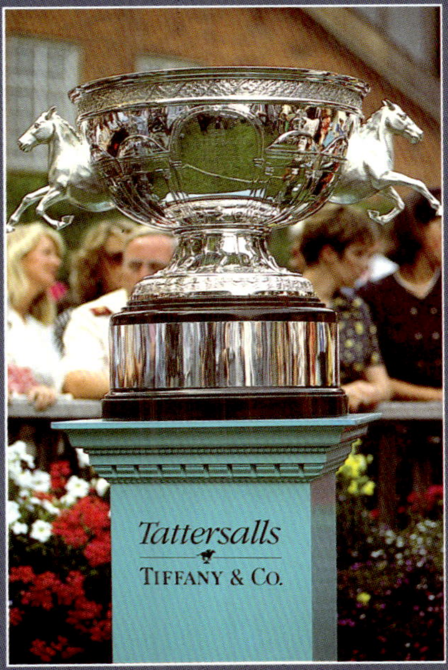
Tattersalls
TIFFANY & Co.

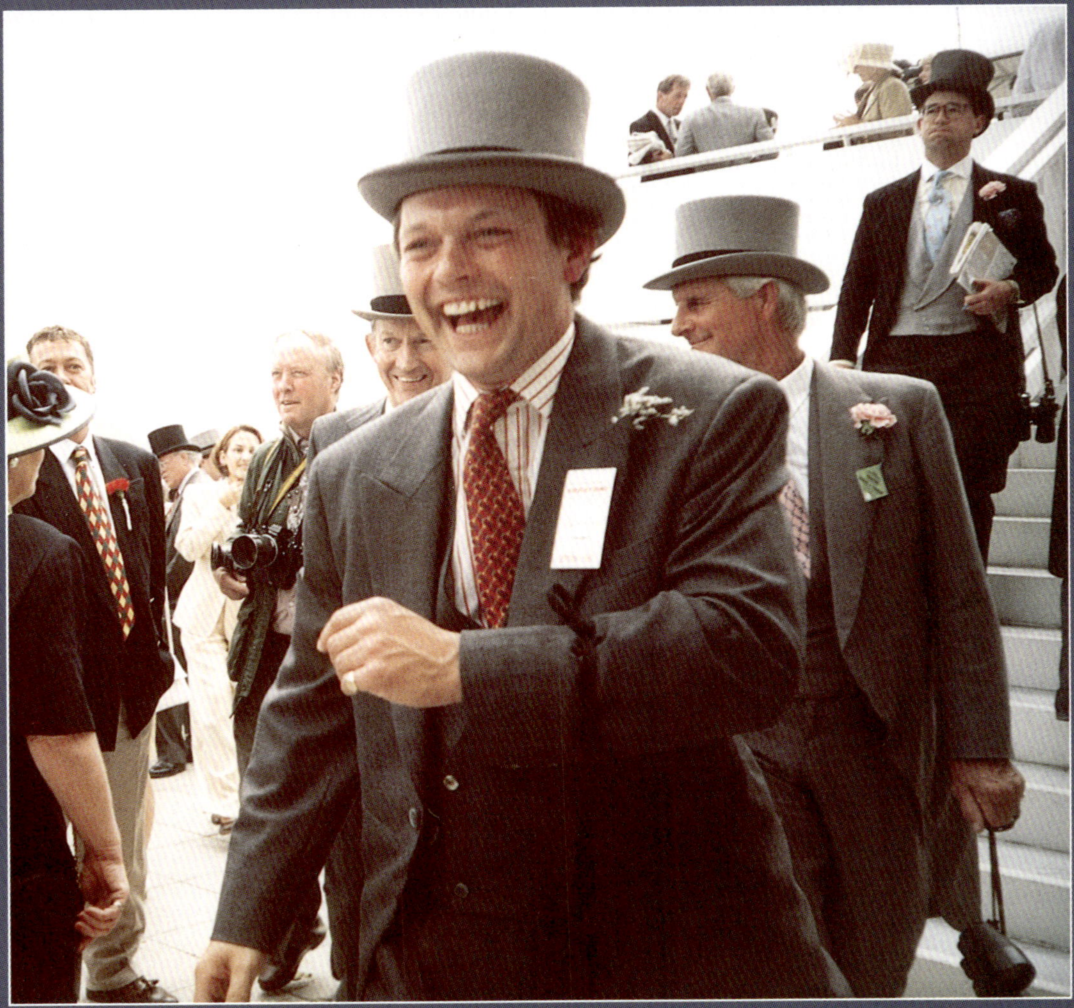

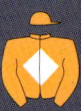

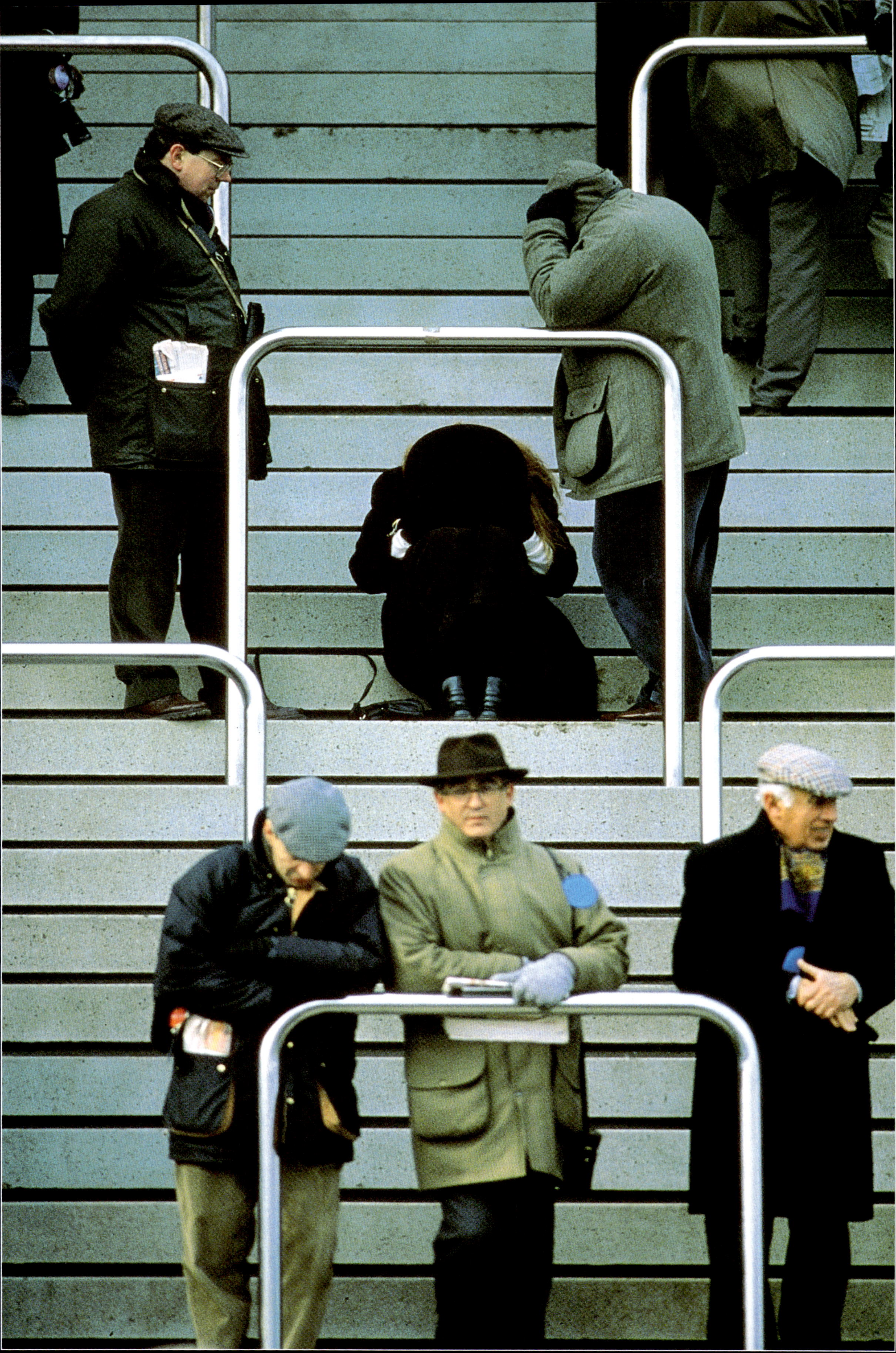

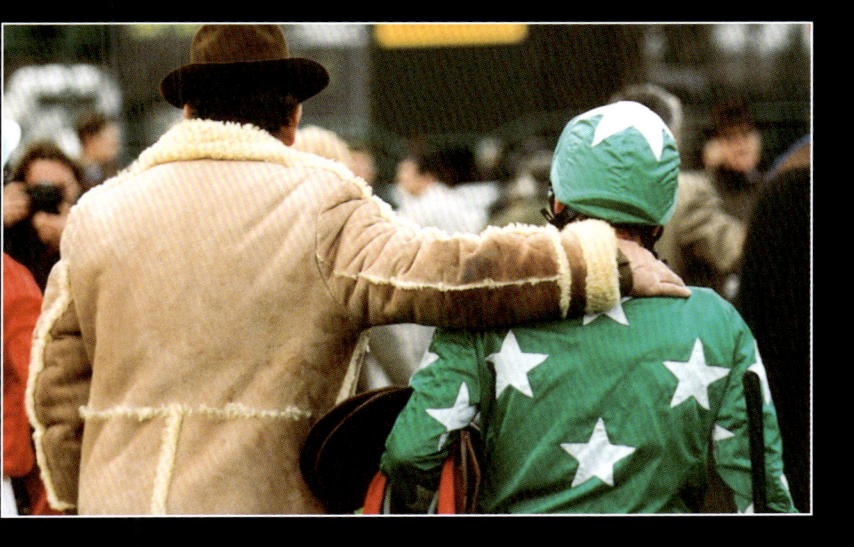

Far Left: Lady Luck lost.
PHOTOGRAPH: ALLSPORT / STU FORSTER.

Top: Beaten but unbowed.
PHOTOGRAPH: JENNIFER UNDERWOOD.

Middle: Consolation.
PHOTOGRAPH: TINA WHITE.

Below: Richard Dunwoody takes a rare tumble.
PHOTOGRAPH: TREVOR JONES.

Next Pages: The long walk.
PHOTOGRAPH: TREVOR JONES.

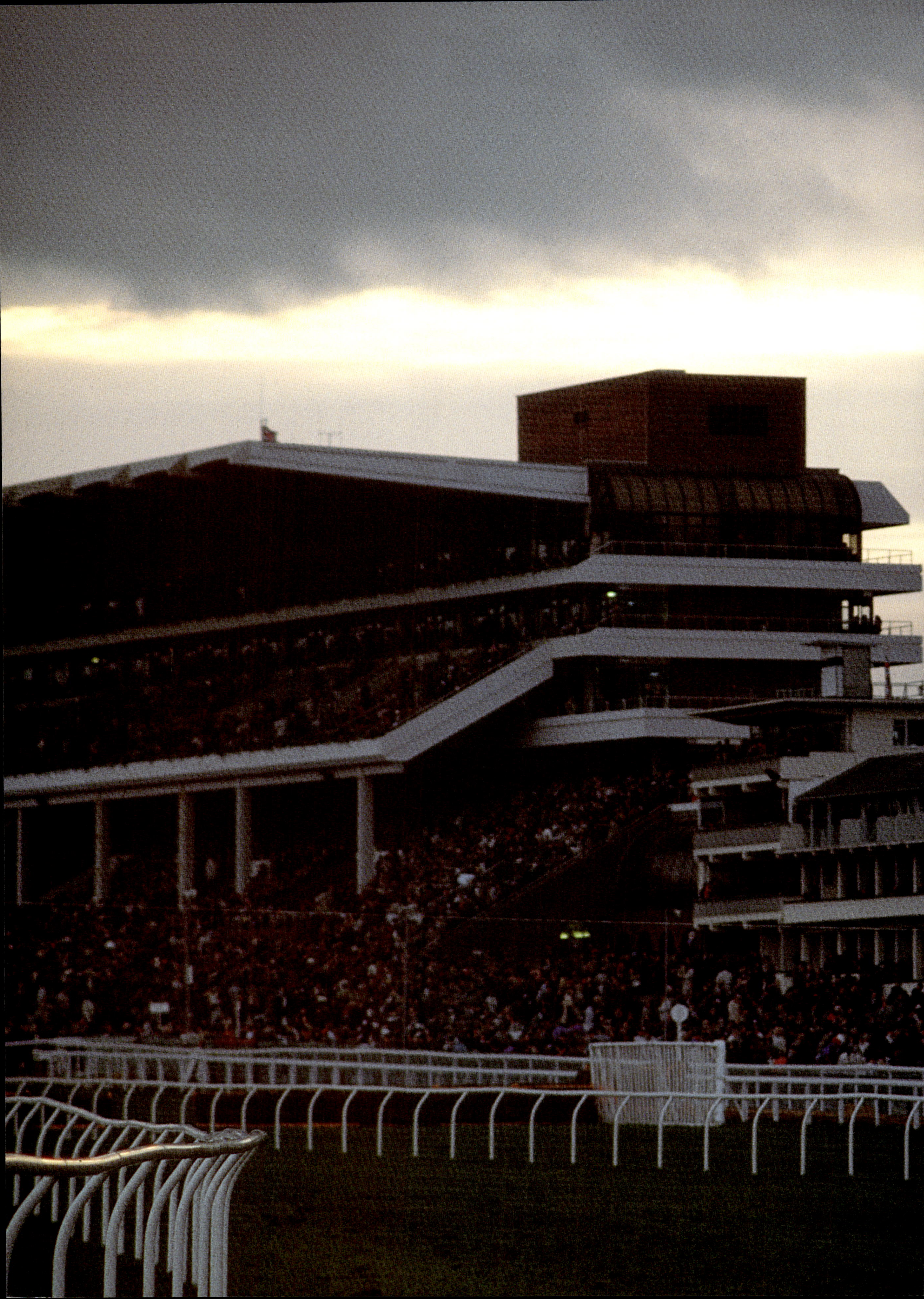

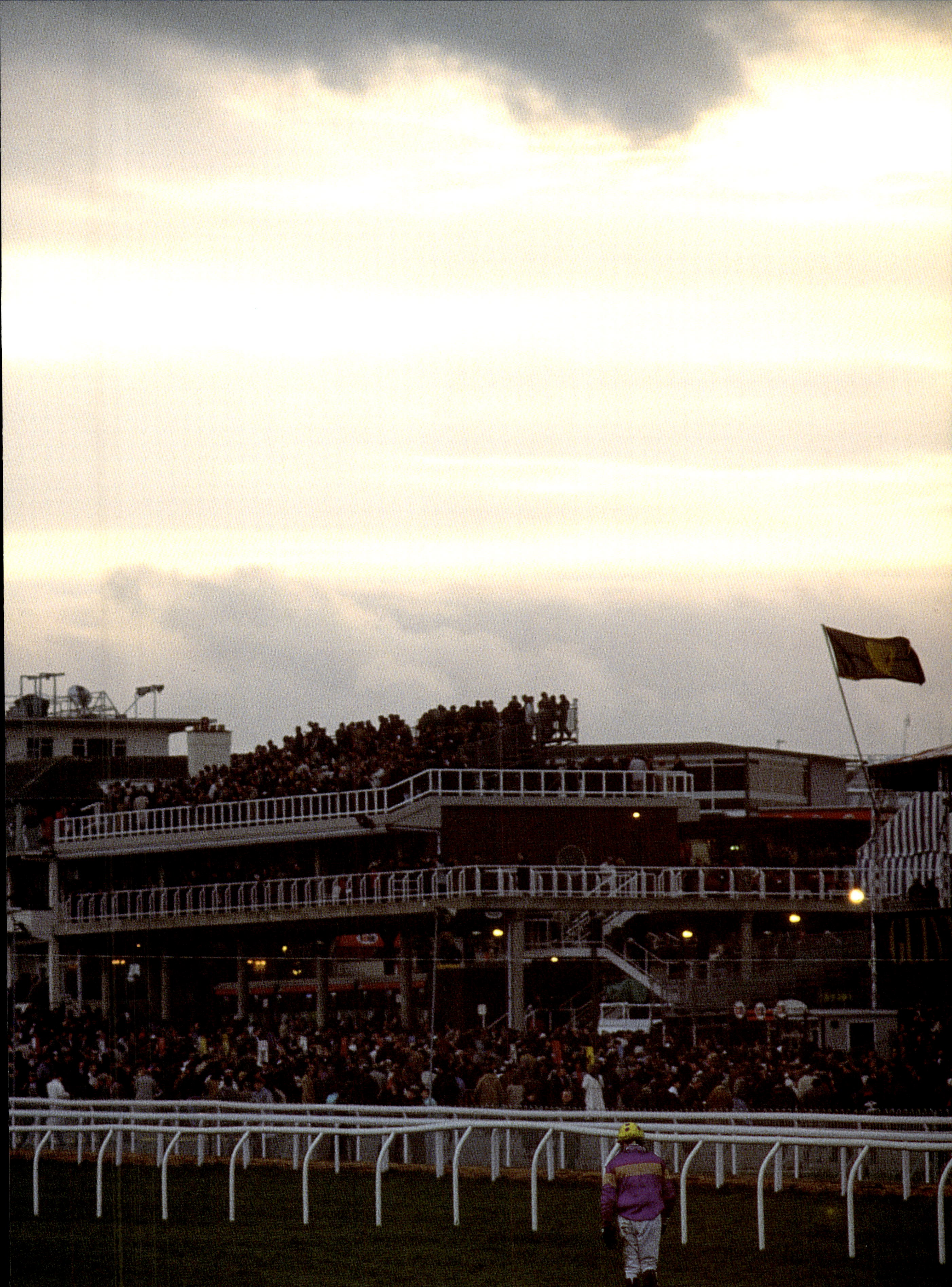

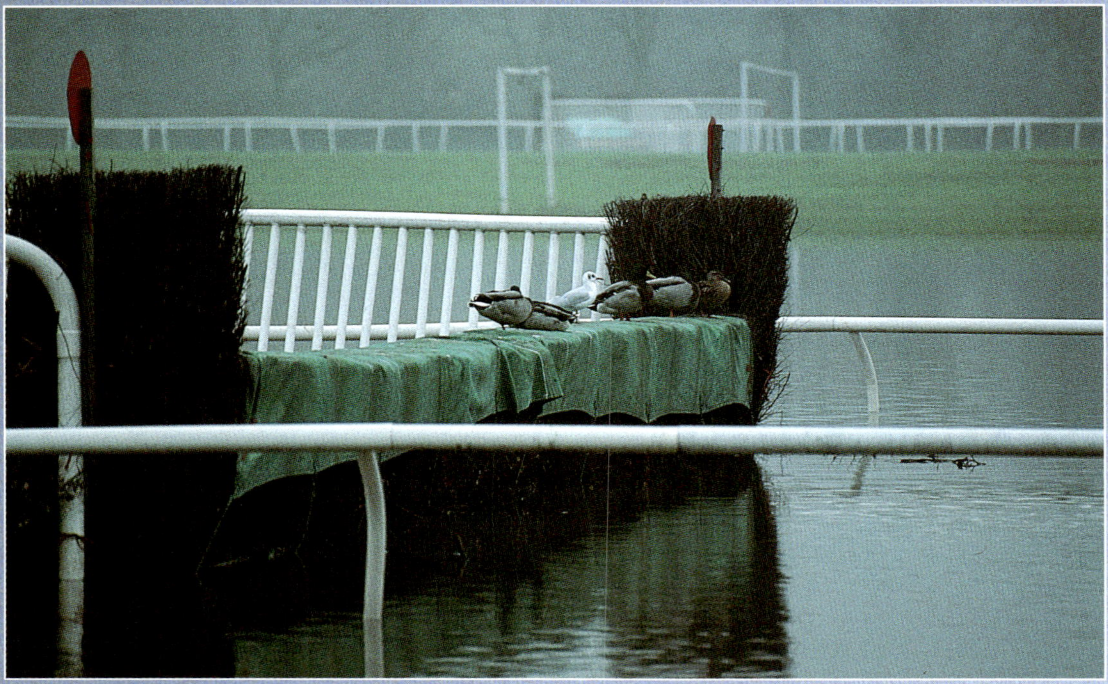

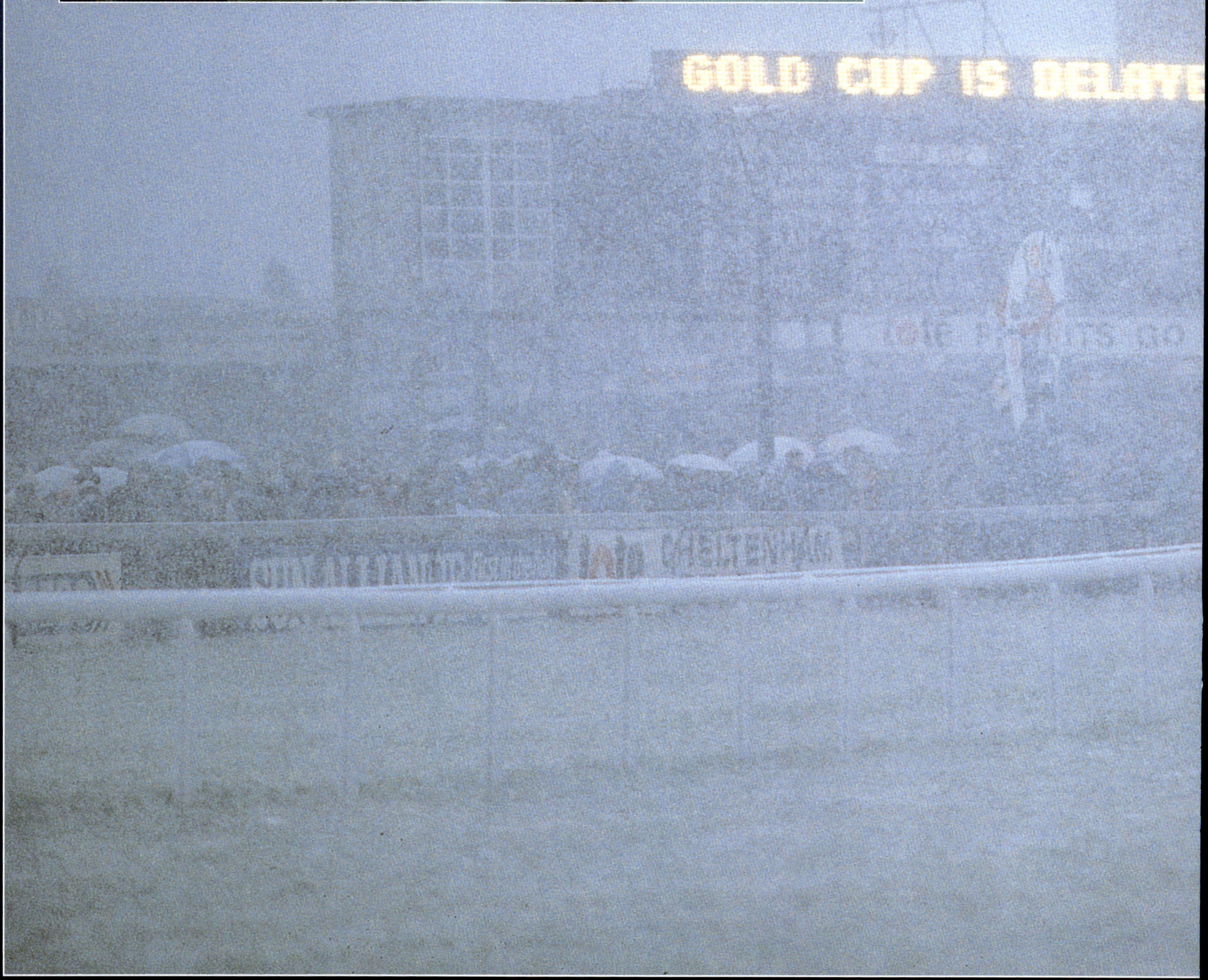
GOLD CUP IS
CHELTENHAM

175

Main photograph: Racing delayed.
PHOTOGRAPH: TREVOR JONES.

Inset: No racing today.
PHOTOGRAPH: IAN YATES.

Melbourne Cup winner Vintage Crop winning the 1993 Jefferson Smurfit Memorial Irish St Leger at the Curragh.
PHOTOGRAPH: ED BYRNE. COURTESY RACING POST.

A World Leader in Packaging

Workmanship from Waterford,
Ireland...

The development of global export markets has created sophisticated demands for packaging which will protect, present and promote a diverse range of products. Fruit and flowers are transported between continents, arriving as fresh as they were picked. Complex electronics need specialised protection for worldwide distribution. Delicate china and glassware must reach distant destinations in perfect condition.

Jefferson Smurfit Group plc has over sixty years' experience in meeting these demands innovatively and cost effectively. Together with its associates, Jefferson Smurfit Group has steadily grown to become the world's largest paper-based packaging organisation and largest recycler of paper, with 400 facilities in over 20 countries throughout Europe, Scandinavia, North and South America, and Asia Pacific.

Smurfit has total control of the packaging manufacturing process, starting with sourcing and sorting waste paper for its own recycling mills, or producing virgin pulp from its own forests, through to the manufacture of paper and board and the production of a broad range of packaging for diverse markets. Throughout its operations worldwide and across its product range, Smurfit applies its commitment to consistently reliable quality and to environmentally responsible production.

From corrugated board to newsprint; sturdy cases to colourful labels; intricate cartons to specialised sacks, Smurfit is skilled in answering the world's packaging needs.

Displayed in Denver,
USA!

JEFFERSON SMURFIT GROUP plc

Worldwide Headquarters:
Clonskeagh, Dublin 4, Ireland.
Phone: (+353 1) 2696622 Fax: (+353 1) 2694481
World Wide Web: htttp://www.smurfit.ie

Smurfit Ireland & UK • Smurfit Continental Europe • Smurfit Latin America • Jefferson Smurfit Corporation USA

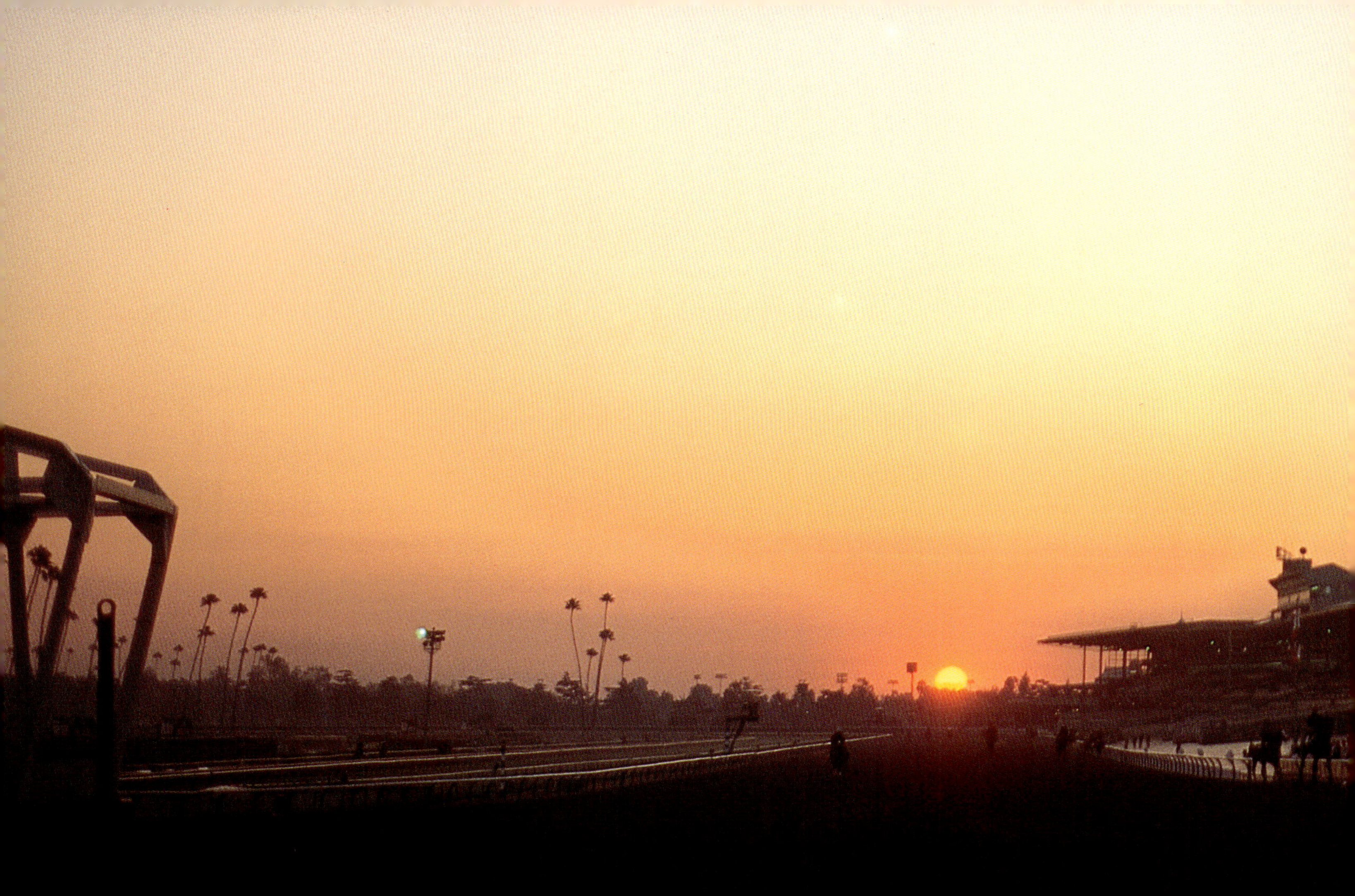

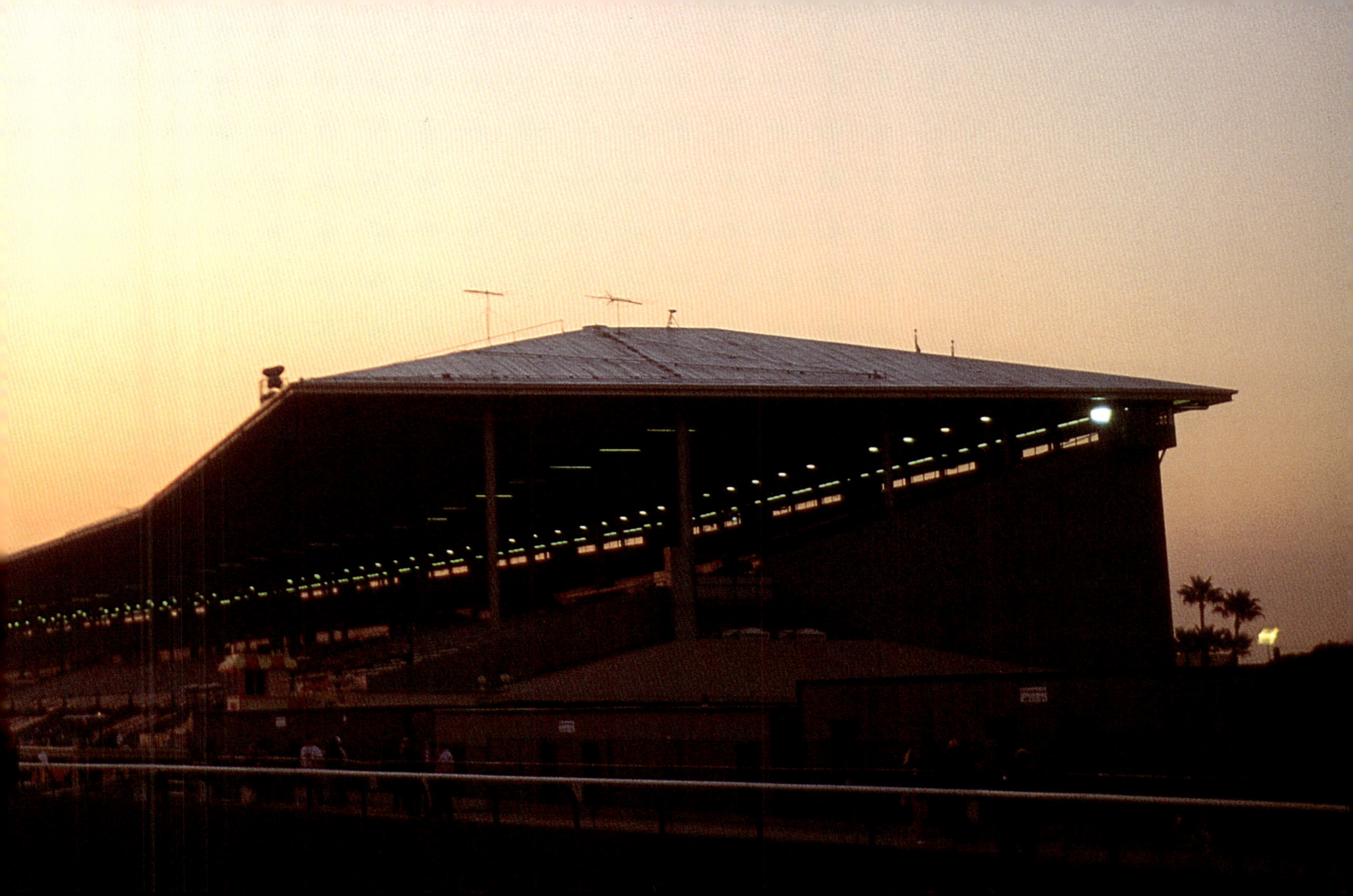

TREVOR JONES
THOROUGHBRED PHOTOGRAPHY
The Hornbeams, 2 The Street, Worlington, Suffolk IP28 8RU
Tel: Newmarket (01638) 713944 Fax (01638) 713945

The stage is quiet.

Waste paper drifts across the Ring. The bars are closing. The rubbish shifters are at work - and maybe a drunk or two. Any chance of a winning ticket? That'll be the day…

Down in the horsebox park, lads and lasses are boxing up - their charges washed down, rugged and bandaged for the long drag home. Some of the lads have a triumph to keep them warm; some disappointment; some through-the-pocket fury at "That moron - calls himself a jockey?"

And just occasionally, hardest of all to forget, there is an empty stall in the back of the box. Old Blacky didn't make it. How the hell are we going to tell Sue? She loved him…

From the other, posher parks, most of the cars are gone - the shrewd 'straight after the last' early birds.

If you've made a day of it, there may still be the remains of the picnic. "Finish the Cherry Brandy? Not on your life. I'm driving…"

A few post-mortems. "Only blew out of the Placepot in the last. That bloody jockey needs an alarm clock."

Doors slam, wheels spin; the lights go on…

The course is silent, waiting for another day.

Previous pages: Santa Anita
PHOTOGRAPH: TREVOR JONES.

Above: A long day at the races.
PHOTOGRAPH: ALLSPORT / SHAUN BOTTERILL

PHOTOGRAPH: ALLSPORT / MIKE HEWITT.

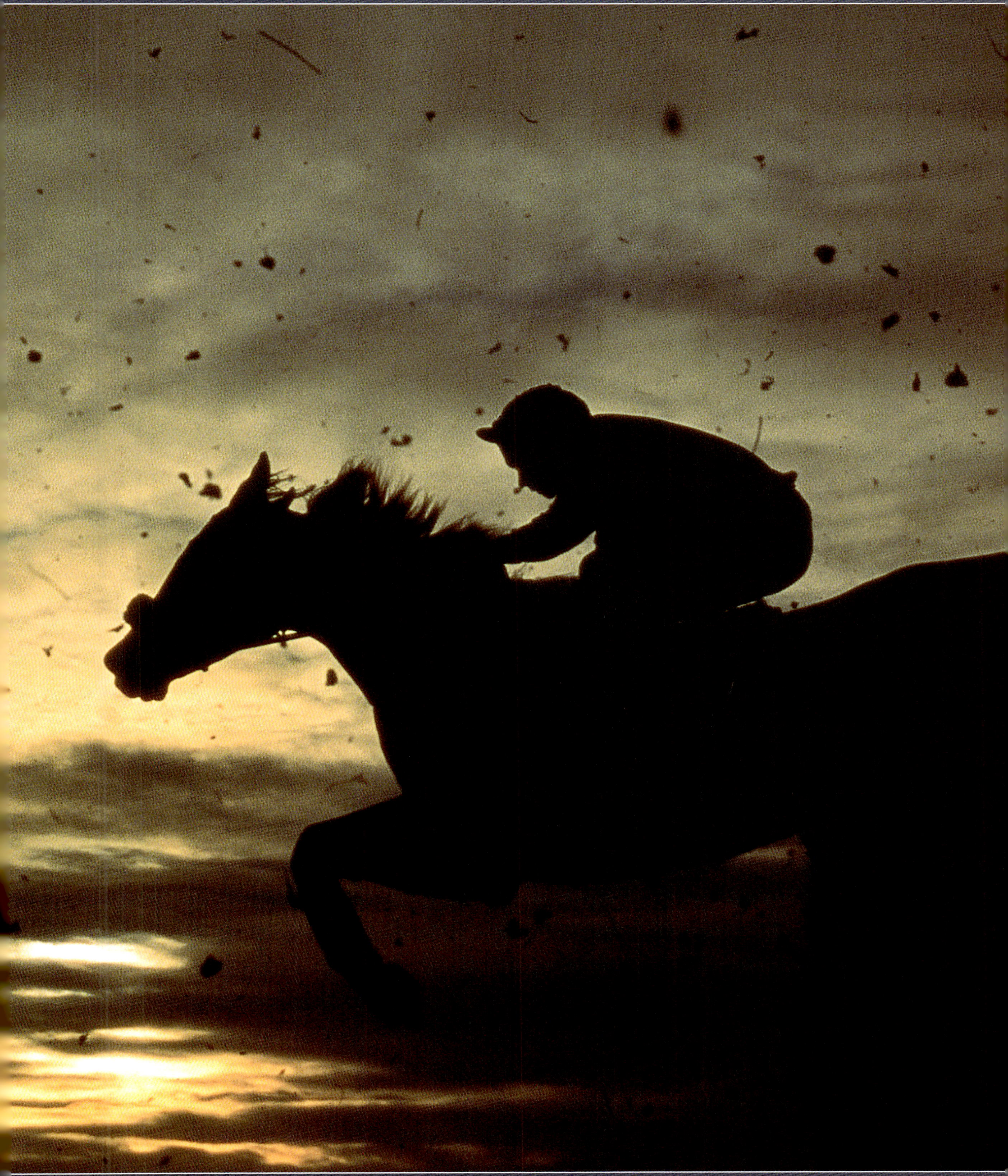

Left: Evening colours.
PHOTOGRAPH: DAVID WALTON.

Below: Starting stalls being towed away at Santa Anita.
PHOTOGRAPH: TREVOR JONES.

INSET PHOTOGRAPH BELOW: TREVOR JONES.

Right: Tokyo racecourse at sundown.
PHOTOGRAPH: ALLSPORT / ANTON WANT.

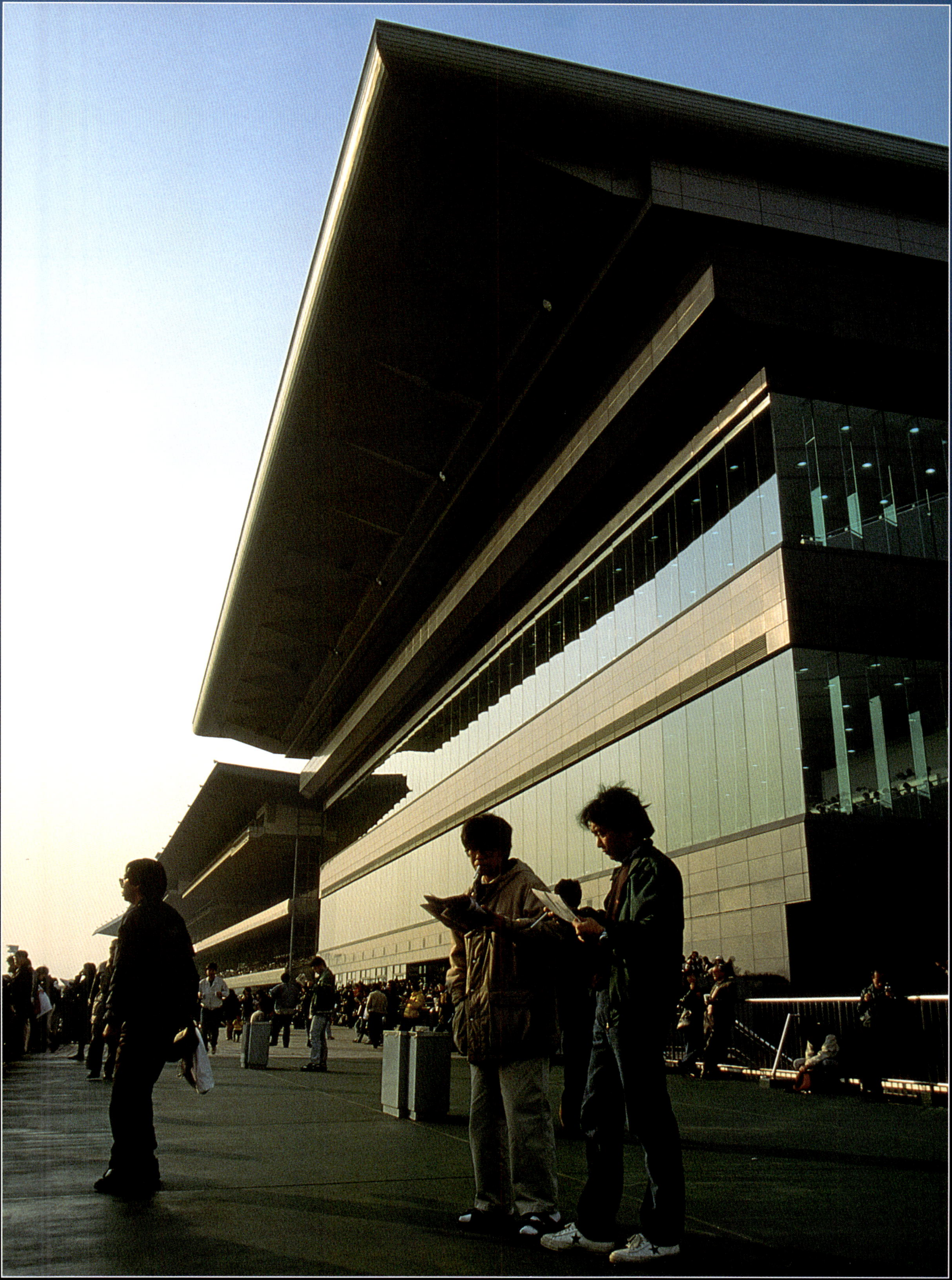

Top Right: Bring on the sweepers.
PHOTOGRAPH: F WHEATLEY.

Bottom Right: 'Saints or Sinners?'
PHOTOGRAPH: S NIXON.

Below: A threatening sky looms over deserted stands at Thirsk.
PHOTOGRAPH: J L SALMOND.

Next pages: At the End of the Day.
PHOTOGRAPH: TERRY VAUGHAN.
(3RD PRIZE IN THE MOODS OF HORSE RACING PHOTOGRAPHIC COMPETITION
AND CHAPTER PRIZE).

187

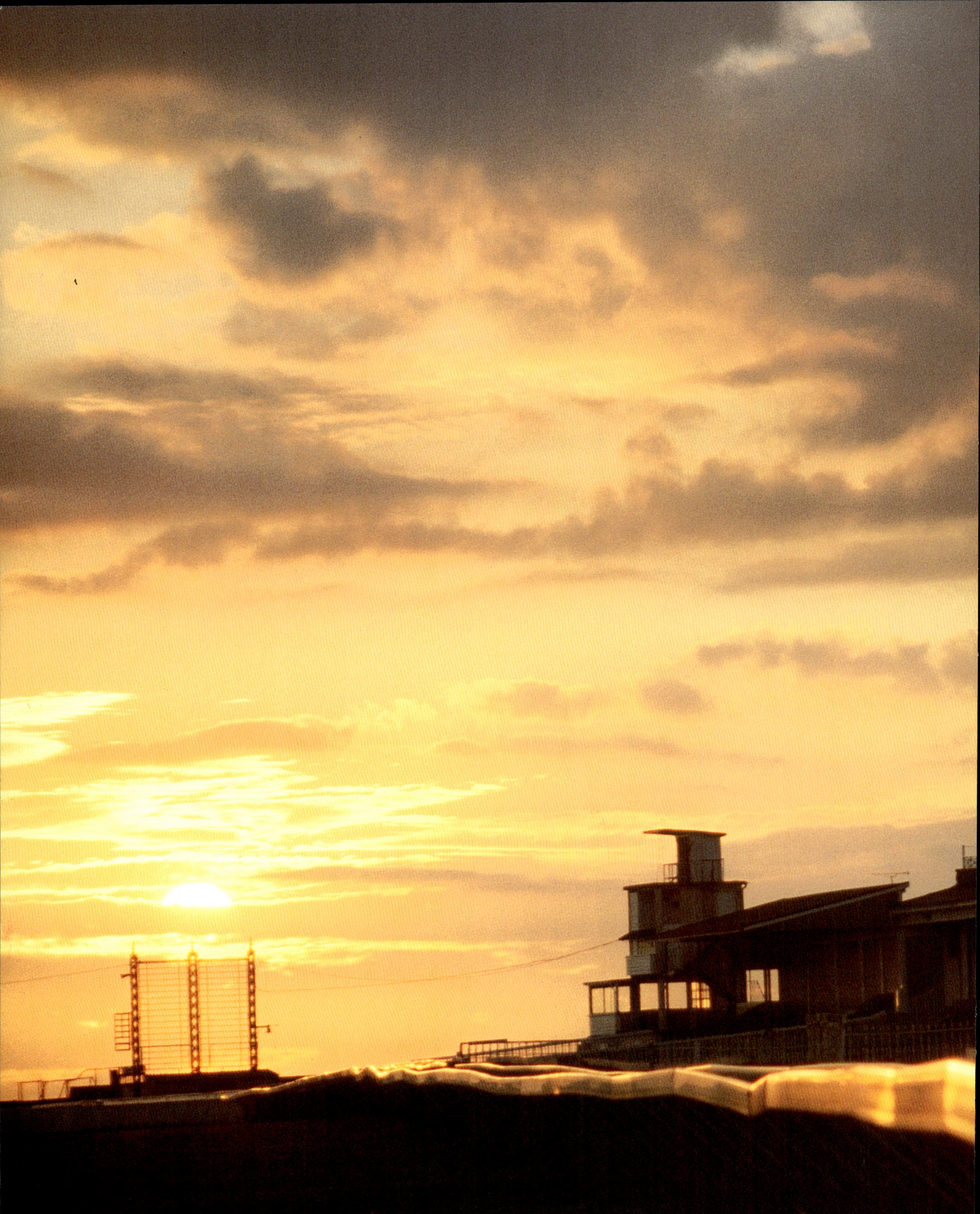

If you're looking for real horsepower, you won't find a safer bet than Saab.

Saab's latest range of technologically advanced engines has been born and bred from a long tradition of Saab engineering excellence. A tradition that combines exceptional power and performance, with a true responsibility for the environment.

That's because Saab drivers demand the very highest standards from the cars they drive. Exclusivity, style, but above all the performance to ensure smooth, safe overtaking in the most demanding of driving conditions.

Combine this with Saab's world renowned standards of safety and of interior refinement and luxury and it's hardly surprising that most pundits in the know would put their money on Saab every time.

For further information on the Saab range and for the details of your nearest Saab dealer call us on:

0800 626556

SAAB

beyond the conventional

the sponsors

The editors wish to thank the following companies who have supported this edition of Moods of Horseracing.

Kim Bailey	The Bloodstock & Stud Investment Co. Ltd. (BASIC)
Cadogan Estates Ltd	Canon (UK) Ltd
Cheveley Park Stud Ltd	Japan Racing Association
Lexmark International Ltd	Marne & Champagne Diffusion (UK)
Olympic Coachbuilders Ltd	Payne & Gunter
Martin Collins Enterprises Ltd	Saab Great Britain Ltd
Smurfit Ltd	The Sporting Life
The Jockey Club	Trevor Jones
United Racecourses (Holdings) Ltd	Victor Chandler Ltd
Vodaphone Group Services Ltd	Weatherbys Group Ltd
	Whitbread Beer Company

Above: Over the sticks.
PHOTOGRAPH: TREVOR JONES.

Previous page: Close racing at Chester.
PHOTOGRAPH: TREVOR JONES.